Making Mortgages Work for You

Other McGraw-Hill Books by Robert Irwin

How to Find Hidden Real Estate Bargains

Handbook of Property Management

Computerizing Your Real Estate Office

The McGraw-Hill Real Estate Handbook

Mingles: A Home Buying Guide for Unmarried Couples (paperback)

Timeshare Properties: What Every Buyer *Must* Know!

Protect Yourself in Real Estate: The Complete Beginner's Guide (paperback)

How to Buy a Home at a Reasonable Price (paperback)

How to Buy and Sell Real Estate for Financial Security (paperback)

Robert Irwin

Making Mortgages Work for You

McGraw-Hill Book Company

New York   St. Louis   San Francisco   Auckland   Bogotá
Hamburg   Johannesburg   London   Madrid   Mexico
Milan   Montreal   New Delhi   Panama
Paris   São Paulo   Singapore
Sydney   Tokyo   Toronto

Library of Congress Cataloging-in-Publication Data

Irwin, Robert
  Making mortgages work for you

  Rev. ed. of: The new mortgage game. c1982.
  Includes index
  1. Mortgage loans—United States. 2. Mortgage
loans, Variable rate—United States. I. Irwin, Robert,
1941–   . New mortgage game. II. Title.
HG2040.5.U5175   1987   332.7′22′0973   86-31270
ISBN 0-07-032129-9

A previous edition of this work was published under the title
The New Mortgage Game.

1234567890   DOC/DOC   893210987

ISBN 0-07-032129-9

*The editors for this book were Martha Jewett and Rita T. Margolies,
the designer was Naomi Auerbach, and the production supervisor
was Annette Mayeski. It was set in Baskerville by Achorn Graphic Services, Inc.*

Printed and bound by R. R. Donnelley & Sons Company.

This book contains the author's opinions. Neither the author nor the publisher is engaged in rendering investment, legal, tax, accounting, or other
similar professional services. If these services are required, the reader should
obtain them from a competent professional. Some material in this book may
be affected by changes in the law (or changes in interpretations of the law) or
may be affected by changes in lending requirements by federal or local lenders since the manuscript was prepared. Therefore, the accuracy and com-
pleteness of information contained in this book and the opinions based on it
are not and cannot be guaranteed. The publisher and the author hereby
specifically disclaim any liability for loss incurred as a consequence of the
advice or information presented in this book.

Contents

Preface

Mortgages are changing. The last time I wrote a book on mortgages (*The New Mortgage Game*) in 1982, interest rates were very high, adjustable rate mortgages (ARMs) were just coming onto the market, and borrowers were in a state of confusion.

Today, interest rates are lower, fixed-rate mortgages have bounced back in popularity, and borrowers are in a state of confusion!

Though times and circumstances have changed, borrowers still have lots of questions about mortgages. Today, however, the questions are different. Today borrowers are asking:

Should I get a 15- or 30-year mortgage?

When does it pay to refinance?

How big a mortgage can I afford? (Based on that mortgage, how high a price can I pay?)

Can I improve my chances of qualifying?

Should I still consider an adjustable rate mortgage?

And many more.

After talking with many borrowers (and would-be borrowers), I have tried to design this book to answer all the questions you are likely to ask.

I think I understand the borrower's perspective. After all, I'm a borrower, too. In the last 5 years I've refinanced my own personal residence 3 times. I've taken out many new loans (as well as assumed existing ones) on properties. All of which is to say that not only do I know where lenders are coming from, but I believe I also know what's vital for you, the borrower, to know and understand to protect yourself and get the best deal.

This book is aimed at borrowers (although lenders will find it extremely useful). My hope is that the few dollars it costs you to purchase, it will save you hundreds if not thousands the next time you buy or refinance real estate.

Robert Irwin

Making Mortgages Work for You

Introduction

In this book we have two basic characters—the borrower and the lender. You already know who the borrower is—it's you! You know what your motivations are.

But, you may not really know much about the lender, about its motivations. Lenders, particularly the large institutional lenders like banks and savings and loan associations, typically like it this way. When we walk into an S&L, we may be greeted with great marble walls, plush carpeting, expensive wood furniture. The people we talk to are courteous, friendly, smiling. The impression we get is that we are dealing with someone who *wants to help us.*

If that's your impression, discard it. The lender is out there to do one thing and one thing only—make money. And you're the pigeon who's going to pay. Take out a pen. Now write this on the palm of your hand. *The lender is the adversary!*

Mutual Benefit

That may seem a bit harsh. After all, isn't a mortgage something of mutual benefit? The lender wants to earn interest on money. We want to borrow so that we can buy or refinance. The mortgage allows each of us to get what we want.

The mutual benefit of a mortgage as just described certainly exists. We need the mortgage just as much as the lender needs it. It does benefit both of us.

Self-Interest

But, having thus disposed of mutual need, let's consider conflicting self-interest. We, as borrowers, want to borrow $100,000. It's to our self-interest to pay the lowest interest rate and to have the most flexible terms.

On the other hand, the lender wants to lend us $100,000. But it's in the lender's self-interest to charge the highest interest rate and to get the least flexible terms. Thus we have two opposing interests: ours and the lender's.

All lenders know this. They also know that most borrowers simply do not recognize the true nature of these conflicting interests. Thus lenders go out of their way to disguise this natural adversary relationship. They put up impressive buildings, hire personable staff, and talk nice.

But none of that changes anything. The lender still wants the highest interest rate and the toughest terms. We want the lowest rate and easiest terms.

Terms

Competition between lenders determines the interest rate on mortgages. We can call around (and I heartily suggest you do—money is money!) to get the best interest rate. You don't need this book to know that a 10 percent mortgage is better than an identical mortgage for 11 percent.

It's when we get to mortgage terms that things get tricky. Lenders understand very clearly *all* the terms of mortgages. They see to it that these terms benefit them.

Borrowers rarely understand the terms of a mortgage (beyond the interest rate). Consequently, borrowers frequently get terms that are not to their advantage.

Terms, like interest rates, are also dictated somewhat by competition. (There is some government regulation here, but not nearly as much as most people believe.) Different lenders offer different terms. In fact, at any given time there is usually a much greater difference between lenders' terms than there is between lenders' interest rates. If the market rate, for example, is 11 percent, almost all lenders will be within ¼ percent of that rate. Their terms, however, may be strikingly different.

A smart and knowledgeable mortgage borrower does not shop just for interest rate. He or she shops also, and perhaps most importantly, for terms.

About This Book

This book explains the terms used in mortgages found around the country. Not just the language, but the conditions of borrowing. It will clearly show you the difference between a "fixed-rate mortgage" and an "adjustable-rate mortgage" (ARM). Then it will take the additional step of explaining which is better and when.

It will cover the stumbling blocks of "assumption" and "prepayment" as well as the real pitfalls of "discounting" and "negative amortization." It will also go into virtually all of the different types of mortgages available to you.

In other words, this book will give you a fighting chance against a lender. After reading this book, you should be able to take on the lenders and come out with not only the best interest rate, but also *the best loan terms* for you.

If you are going after a mortgage and you don't have the information that's in this book, you're walking into a boxing ring with both hands tied behind your back. If you do know what's in this book, you're going in like a contender . . . and you could come out the champ.

1
How Big a Mortgage Can You Afford?

The good thing about buying real estate is that most of the purchase price can be financed with a mortgage. The bad thing is that we must pay that mortgage back.

Thus, although the down payment is important, very often the real determinant of which home or property we can buy is a matter of how big a mortgage we can afford. The bigger the mortgage, the bigger the property. The smaller the mortgage, the smaller the purchase. If you're reading this book, chances are "size of mortgage" is one of the things you're wondering about. How big a mortgage can you personally afford, and what are the best terms you can get? We'll cover mortgage size in this chapter and the best terms to look for in the remainder of the book.

What Determines the Maximum Mortgage You Can Borrow

John might think, perhaps correctly, that he can afford payments of $1000 a month. His calculation is based on what he makes, his current housing expenses, and maybe some money saved from his food allowance. However, if John decides to purchase a house which requires a big mortgage on it, no mortgage lender (such as a bank or savings and loan) is going to ask him, "What do you think you can afford to pay a month?"

Rather, the lender is going to look at his finances, his credit history, the house and down payment, *and then tell John what payments he can afford!* To put it another way, the lender will determine the maximum mortgage John or anyone else can afford according to strict rules and guidelines.

Thus, for practical purposes, the real questions become: What are the lender's guidelines, and what do they say we can afford? Of course, we could differ with the lender's opinion. We might feel we could afford to pay higher (or lower) monthly payments. But our feelings really won't count with lenders. They are hard-nosed business people who look strictly at the facts.

The Guidelines Lenders Follow

Let's assume that we are considering the purchase of a residence in which to live. (The guidelines for investment property are somewhat different and will be covered later.) We need to finance the majority of the purchase price, so we approach a lender, a savings and loan association. What does the S&L look for?

Essentially there are three categories that the S&L looks at:

1. Down payment
2. Borrower's credit history
3. Borrower's ability to repay

Down Payment

There are all kinds of mortgages, as we'll see, and they require different down payments. They run the extreme from Veterans Guaranteed loans for which no down payment is required to loans on bare land, where traditionally a 50 percent down payment is needed.

For our purposes we'll forget about government-guaranteed (VA) or -insured (FHA) loans for the moment (they're covered in later chapters), and we won't worry about land loans. Instead we'll concentrate on the standard "conventional" (nongovernment) mortgage. Here we usually have only two choices. A down payment of 10 percent of the purchase price typically with the seller carrying back a 10 percent second (although a 90 percent first mortgage is a possibility) or a down payment of 20 percent or more of the purchase price. (As little as 5 percent down can be a possibility under special circumstances with Private Mortgage Insurance, which also will be discussed later.)

Thus, if we're buying a home for $100,000, our down payment typically will be *either* $10,000 or $20,000. But, you may ask: Why the choice? Why the two different downs?

The answer is that lenders use different qualifying formulas depending on the down payment. As we'll see shortly, it's *easier* to qualify for a mortgage when you put $20,000 down than it is if you only put $10,000 down.

Special note: Some lenders offer "no-qualifying" mortgages if the buyer puts 25 percent or more down on the property. In this case, as long as the property appraises out at the purchase price, the borrower does not need to qualify in any way. (There are usually a higher interest rate and more "points" for this type of loan.)

Credit History

After the down payment, the next thing a lender looks at is our credit history. Today, houses cost a lot of money. Typically a buyer will want to borrow $50,000, $100,000, $150,000, or more. That's a lot, and any lender is going to want some assurance that the borrower intends to pay it back.

What makes lenders feel comfortable is a good credit history on the part of the borrower. A credit history means evidence that we've borrowed and repaid "as agreed" many times before. Thus the lender will order a credit check on us.

Note: Having a good credit history is different from having *no* credit history. Some people think it's a good idea to pay cash for everything and not bother with credit cards. That's bad when it comes time to get a mortgage. If a lender orders a credit check and it comes back a blank sheet of paper, the lender has nothing on which to base an estimate of credit, hence the mortgage may be turned down. Remember, sometimes no credit is just as bad as bad credit.

A good credit report will show a dozen different accounts we've opened in recent years. They might include Visa or MasterCard, gas or department store credit cards, or loans we've taken out. The more the merrier as long as after each one there's the comment *"paid as agreed."*

Ability to Repay

Finally, the most critical factor determining how big a mortgage we can afford is our ability to repay—in other words, our income. Our income will ultimately determine the highest mortgage we can afford.

In general, lenders will allow us a maximum monthly payment based on our monthly income. (The maximum monthly payment determines the maximum size of the mortgage.) The basic formula that most lenders use is that the *total* monthly payment cannot exceed 36 percent of our total monthly income. To understand this formula, however, we need to know what goes into "total monthly payment." It includes the following:

Mortgage principal

Mortgage interest

Property taxes and insurance

Other long-term debt

The last item, other long-term debt, is often a stumbling block for many would-be borrowers. It includes car payments, credit card payments, bank loans—any debt that runs for a term of 6 to 8 months or longer. Thus, if our mortgage payment (principal, interest, taxes, and insurance) comes to $500 a month, an income of $2000 should easily cover it. However, if we also are paying an additional $1000 a month in long-term debt, then our total payment comes to $1500 a month and our income will not come close to covering it.

Since everyone's long-term debt is different (some people pay cash and have *no* long-term debt), it has become more convenient to simply speak in terms of the "net" monthly payment. This is just the principal, interest, taxes, and insurance on the property. Lenders use separate formulas for these as we will see in the next section. It is important to remember, however, that to qualify, a borrower must generally fulfill *both* the following formulas as well as the "36 percent" rule just described.

Determining Maximum Net Monthly Payment from Income

The maximum net monthly payment we can afford is determined by simple formulas that most lenders use. These formulas depend on the size of the down payment. (Remember, we said the down payment could be either 10 or 20 percent.) *In general,* the formulas used are these:

> *If we put 10 percent down, then our monthly payment* (including mortgage, taxes, and insurance) *cannot exceed 29 percent of our income.* (Many lenders set a maximum of 28 percent.)

For 10 percent down, multiply monthly income by 0.29 to get the maximum monthly payment a lender will allow.

> *If we put 20 percent down, then our monthly payment cannot exceed 33 percent of our income.* (Many lenders set a maximum of 32 percent.)

For 20 percent down, multiply monthly income by 0.33 for the maximum monthly payment a lender will allow.

For example, John's income is $2260. At 10 percent down his maximum monthly payment is 29 percent of that (0.29 × $2260), or $655. However, if John puts 20 percent down, his maximum monthly payment moves up to 33 percent of $2260, or $745. That's $90 more . . . and could make the difference between being able to buy a place or not.

John's Maximum Monthly Payment

	10 percent down	20 percent down
Monthly income	$2260	$2260
Multiply by	0.29	0.33
Maximum net monthly payment	$ 655	$ 745

Why Lenders Use Different Formulas

Why do lenders use different percentages depending on the down payment? A lot has to do with commitment. They figure that a person who puts 20 percent down is a lot more committed to making the payments than a person who only puts 10 percent down. Thus they are more willing to loan such a person a higher percentage of his or her net income.

Additionally, most lenders turn around and sell a good many of the loans they make on the secondary market to government agencies such as Fannie Mae or Freddie Mac. (These agencies buy loans from lenders, thus giving lenders money to go out and make new loans.) For the lender to be able to sell them, the loans must fall within the agencies' guidelines, which involve the "29 and 33 percent rule" just discussed.

Converting Maximum Monthly Payment to Maximum Loan Amount

We've gone over the basic requirements you must meet to get a new mortgage from an S&L or a bank. Assuming you have good credit and are putting 10 or 20 percent down, how big a monthly payment can you afford? Based on the monthly payment, how big a mortgage can you get?

Calculating this is just a little bit tricky because the maximum payment is supposed to include not only mortgage payment (principal and interest), but also taxes and insurance. Yet taxes and insurance will vary from property to property.

As a rule of thumb, therefore, we'll assume that taxes and insurance are going to equal 2 percent of the purchase price. That will be a bit high for states such as California which have very low property taxes, and a bit low for states such as Minnesota which have higher taxes. Depending on the tax rate in your state you'll need to adjust the mortgage amount up or down a little bit.

In addition the maximum mortgage for any given maximum monthly payment will differ depending on the interest rate. For example, you could expect to get twice as much mortgage at 6 percent interest as you could at 12 percent.

To solve these different problems, yet give you, the reader, a reasonably good basic guide that you can use, we'll use the following chart for 10 percent down.

How to Determine the Maximum Mortgage You Can Afford (and the Maximum House Price) If You Know Your Net Income

From Table 1.1 and the tables in the Appendix you should be able to very quickly determine the maximum mortgage (and house price) you can afford.

Hint: Interest rates vary a bit from lender to lender. Call a few savings and loan associations to get an idea of what their current rates are. When you call, ask for the rate for 30-year "fixed loans." This is the true market rate. Do not accept the rate for ARMs (adjustable-rate mortgages) because this usually includes a temporary discount which will be discussed in Chapter 4.

Other Considerations

What we've learned how to do is calculate the maximum mortgage we can get. Of course, there are other considerations. They might include:

Points. A charge for getting the loan which lenders add on. One point equals 1 percent of the loan amount.

Type of loan. Whether we should get an ARM or fixed-rate or some other variety.

Term of loan. Shorter-term loans, those for 15 years instead of 30, typically carry slightly lower interest rates. Should we opt for these?

Table 1.1. Approximate Maximum 30-Year Mortgage Available at Different Incomes

10 Percent Down Payment. 15 Percent of the Monthly Payment Will Go toward Taxes and Insurance

Monthly income	Interest rate charged on mortgage						
	9%	10%	11%	12%	13%	14%	15%
$1500	$45,952	$44,611	$38,825	$35,946	$33,425	$31,206	$29,242
1600	49,016	47,585	41,414	38,342	35,653	33,286	31,191
1700	52,079	50,559	44,002	40,739	37,882	35,366	33,141
1800	55,143	53,534	46,591	43,135	40,110	37,447	35,090
1900	58,206	56,508	49,179	45,531	42,338	39,527	37,040
2000	61,270	59,482	51,767	47,928	44,567	41,608	38,989
2100	64,333	62,456	54,356	50,324	46,795	43,688	40,939
2200	67,397	65,430	56,944	52,721	49,023	45,768	42,888
2300	70,460	68,404	59,532	55,117	51,252	47,849	44,838
2400	73,524	71,378	62,121	57,513	53,480	49,929	46,787
2500	76,587	74,352	64,709	59,910	55,708	52,009	48,737
2600	79,651	77,326	67,297	62,306	57,937	54,090	50,686
2700	82,714	80,300	69,886	64,703	60,165	56,170	52,636
2800	85,777	83,274	72,474	67,099	62,393	58,251	54,585
2900	88,841	86,249	75,062	69,495	64,622	60,331	56,534
3000	91,904	89,223	77,651	71,892	66,850	62,411	58,484
3100	94,968	92,197	80,239	74,288	69,078	64,492	60,433
3200	98,031	95,171	82,828	76,685	71,307	66,572	62,383
3300	101,095	98,145	85,416	79,081	73,535	68,653	64,332
3400	104,158	101,119	88,004	81,477	75,763	70,733	66,282
3500	107,222	104,093	90,593	83,874	77,992	72,813	68,231
3600	110,285	107,067	93,181	86,270	80,220	74,894	70,181
3700	113,349	110,041	95,769	88,666	82,448	76,974	72,130
3800	116,412	113,015	98,358	91,063	84,677	79,054	74,080
3900	119,476	115,989	100,946	93,459	86,905	81,135	76,029
4000	122,539	118,964	103,534	95,856	89,133	83,215	77,979
4100	125,603	121,938	106,123	98,252	91,361	85,296	79,928
4200	128,666	124,912	108,711	100,648	93,590	87,376	81,877
4300	131,730	127,886	111,300	103,045	95,818	89,456	83,827
4400	134,793	130,860	113,888	105,441	98,046	91,537	85,776
4500	137,857	133,834	116,476	107,838	100,275	93,617	87,726
4600	140,920	136,808	119,065	110,234	102,503	95,697	89,675
4700	143,984	139,782	121,653	112,630	104,731	97,778	91,625
4800	147,047	142,756	124,241	115,027	106,960	99,858	93,574
4900	150,111	145,730	126,830	117,423	109,188	101,939	95,524
5000	153,174	148,704	129,418	119,820	111,416	104,019	97,473

These and other considerations will be dealt with in the next chapters.

Worksheet

Use the following worksheet to determine your maximum mortgage amount:

Income	\$_____
× 0.29 or 0.33	
(depending on down)	×_____
Maximum net monthly payment	_____
Income	\$_____
× 0.36	×0.36 _____
Maximum net monthly payment plus long term debt	_____

2

The Difference between "Fixed"-Rate Mortgages and "ARMs"

In the mortgage marketplace today there is a wide variety of home loans available, probably several hundred different kinds. However, they all can be grouped into two broad categories: the "fixed-rate mortgage" and the "adjustable-rate mortgage" (or ARM).

The basic difference between these two types of mortgages is quite simple to understand. For a *fixed-rate* mortgage the interest rate remains the same for the life of the loan. (*Note:* For purposes of illustration we'll use the terms "mortgage" and "loan" interchangeably.) With an *ARM* the interest rate floats up or down.

Perhaps an example will clarify any lingering confusion for those new to the mortgage game. We obtain a mortgage of $100,000 at 10 percent interest per year for 30 years. If this is a fixed-rate loan, our interest will remain at 10 percent for the full 30-year term.

On the other hand, if this is an ARM, our interest rate may fluctuate up (for example to 12 percent) or down (for example to 8 percent) over the term of the loan. The interest rate charged on an ARM is adjusted up or down at regular intervals.

Advantages of the Fixed Rate

The principal advantage of a fixed-rate mortgage is that we always know where we stand. If our interest rate is 12 percent and our payments are $1000 a month, they are not going to change. They will be the same at year 5 or at year 30. There is great peace of mind in such knowledge.

Also, as times goes by, chances are our income will grow. As our income goes up, we will have to devote less and less of it to the fixed monthly payment. As a result we will feel, and actually be getting, richer!

Finally, if we get a fixed-rate mortgage at a time when interest rates are low and interest rates rise later, we are protected. Our interest rate remains at the original (now low) level.

Advantages of the ARM

The principal advantage of an ARM, on the other hand, is its *availability*. In times of volatile interest rates, such as the period between 1980 and 1984, lenders such as savings and loan associations and banks were afraid to lend money long term. They didn't want to commit themselves to a 30-year real estate loan when they had no idea where interest rates would be even 6 months into the future.

Thus, while banks were quoting *fixed rates* of 17 percent (to protect themselves), they were also quoting ARMs at 13 percent. They felt comfortable with the ARM because they knew that if interest rates in general rose, the rate on the ARM would also rise. Thus, when fixed-rate loans are difficult or impossible to find, ARMs are usually plentiful.

This leads us to the second advantage of an ARM. As an inducement to the buyer to take this type of mortgage, the lender will typically offer a discount—often initially knocking off several points (a point is 1 percent of interest) from the market rate. *If we are only planning to hold the property for a year or two* (perhaps as an investment), then we can take advantage of this discount. We get the ARM with the below-market interest rate, and then later, when the interest rate is adjusted upward, we either sell the property or refinance.

For example, a friend of mine was able to turn the initial discount on an ARM to his advantage this way: He purchased a home in 1984 and was given a choice of an ARM with an introductory rate of 9½ percent or a fixed-rate mortgage at 13½ percent. He selected the ARM.

The rate on the ARM was adjusted upward by a maximum of 2 percent a year. Thus by 1986 it could have reached 13½ percent. However, during that time interest rates fell, and in 1986 my friend refinanced to a

9½ percent fixed-rate loan. During those 2 years the highest interest rate he paid was 11½ percent and his average rate was 10½ percent.

On the other hand, if he had opted for the fixed-rate mortgage, during those 2 years before he refinanced he would have paid a flat 13½ percent. By taking advantage of the ARM's low introductory rate and because he was able to refinance in a low interest rate market 2 years later, he saved himself 2 percent interest over the period. Considering that the loan amount was $150,000, that amounted to a cash savings of $3000 per year or a total of $6000 in interest saved!

Disadvantages of the Fixed Rate

The biggest disadvantage of fixed-rate loans today is that they are, in general, not assumable. (VA and FHA loans are an exception.) We may get a great 10 percent fixed-rate loan, and a few years later mortgage rates may rise to 14 percent.

Here we are sitting with our wonderful 10 percent rate. We decide to sell, thinking we have a real selling feature, only to discover that the loan is written in such a way that it all becomes due and payable the moment we sell. Yes, we get the benefit of the 10 percent while we own the property. But the next buyer can't.

Disadvantages of the ARM

ARMs are frequently assumable. However, most people aren't interested in assuming them because of their one very great disadvantage. With an ARM we seldom know what our interest rate *or our monthly payment* will be in the future. We may be paying 12 percent and $1000 a month today. But next year we could be paying 14 percent and $1200 a month.

If we are struggling just to make our current monthly payment (as many home buyers are), then having a sudden wrenching adjustment upward in the payment can be catastrophic. It could cause us to default on the payments, to lose the property.

Additionally, in a rising interest rate market, the rate on an ARM will typically rise along with other interest rates. Thus, we don't get the benefits of keeping a low interest rate mortgage in a high interest rate market.

Other Facts about ARMs

A Faulty Comparison

Some lenders are quick to point out another supposed advantage of an ARM over a fixed rate. With an ARM, when interest rates go *down,* the ARM goes down as well. With a fixed rate, when interest rates go down, we are stuck with our now *high* fixed-rate mortgage. Thus the ARM has the advantage.

In theory this argument makes sense. In practice, however, it is vacuous. When interest rates go down, those with fixed rate mortgages as well as those with ARMs typically refinance to a lower fixed rate. Thus the fixed rate offers the same advantage here as the ARM.

Making the ARM Safer?

Lenders are aware of borrowers' fears of unlimited interest rate hikes on ARMs. If the mortgage were allowed to rise indefinitely, in a very volatile market we might start up paying 10 percent and end up paying 20 percent! Few borrowers would take out a mortgage with such a possibility written into it.

To help reduce borrowers' fears, lenders frequently put "caps" on the interest rate. The rate, for example, might be allowed to rise 5 percent above the original rate *but no more.* Thus, we know that if our loan starts at 10 percent, it can never get higher than 15 percent, and that our payments therefore can rise only to a certain limit (a maximum increase of 50 percent in this case).

Since payments are usually more important to borrowers than interest rates, some lenders put caps on the payments. However, if only the payment is capped and not the interest rate, we can get "negative amortization," which means we can end up owing more than we originally borrowed! This will be discussed in greater detail in a later chapter.

My own feeling is that caps do help, but do not solve the basic problem with ARMs. We still can't know what the future will hold with an ARM.

Easier Qualifying?

Another frequently quoted advantage of an ARM is that it is easier to "qualify" for, and it is easier to get. For example, suppose that interest rates for fixed-rate loans are 12 percent and the payment on ours would be $1000 per month. Also suppose that the introductory rate for an ARM is 10 percent with a monthly payment of $850. It is far easier to qualify for an $850 monthly payment than for a $1000 one. Often a home buyer who can't qualify for a fixed-rate loan can qualify for an ARM being offered at a lower introductory interest rate. Thus the only way to make a purchase in this case may be to get the ARM.

The problem, of course, is that the low ARM rate is *introductory*. Within a short while it can rise to the market rate of 12 percent (in the case cited above) and, correspondingly, the monthly payments can soon rise to $1000. Thus the benefit is short-lived. (*Note:* This problem is the subject of an important discussion in Chapter 4.)

Once again, the supposed benefit of the ARM may turn into a serious drawback at a later date.

Opinion

In my opinion, an ARM is a gamble. It can make sense in a high interest rate market *if* interest rates subsequently fall (see the story above). It can also make sense if you resell or refinance within a few years, having taken advantage of a low introductory rate.

For the long haul, however, I believe an ARM is a mortgage to stay away from, because it shifts the burden of dealing with volatile interest rates from the lender to the borrower. With an ARM the lender can sleep at night without worrying if rates will rise. But can the borrower make a similar claim?

How ARMs Really Work

The features of fixed-rate mortgages are straightforward and simple. ARMs, however, tend to be complex and easily misunderstood. Therefore, the discussion in the remainder of this chapter and that of the following two chapters concerns the various ramifications of ARMs for the borrower.

Indexing

The most obvious feature of an ARM is that it is indexed. What this means is that the interest rate of the ARM is tied to some well-known index. If the index rises, the ARM's interest rate will rise. If the index falls, the rate on the ARM will fall.

If we are borrowing money, it is essential that we know *which index the mortgage is tied to*. Of course we will want to follow the index ourselves. But more importantly, we will usually want to be sure that we select a lender who uses an index that is *as stable as possible*.

If the index fluctuates wildly, then we may end up with payments that

soar one year and fall the next. For most borrowers wide monthly payment fluctuations are very hard to handle.

The Most Commonly Used Indices

The Office of the Comptroller of the Currency (which regulates bank-
ing) and the Federal Home Loan Bank Board (which regulates savings
and loan associations) do not specify which index a lender must use.
Rather, it is up to the lender to make this selection. The regulators only
specify that the index must be one over which the lender has no control,
that it reflect interest rates in general, and that it be widely publicized.

The most commonly used indices are:

1. Six-month T-bill yields
2. One-year T-bill yields
3. Three-year T-bill yields
4. Cost of funds for FHLBB (usually Eleventh District)
5. Cost of fixed-rate mortgages (long-term)

Of these five, the most commonly used are number 2, the 1-year
Treasury security, and number 4, the cost of funds for the Eleventh
District FHLBB. Each of these indices is explained along with a chart
showing the activity of each index for the past 20 years.

T-Bill Rates

These indices show the rate to investors who buy Treasury securities
with terms ranging from 6 months to 3 years. The index is based on
yields. (See Figs. 2.1 to 2.3.)

Cost of Funds for S&Ls

This is the rate that savings and loan associations pay when they borrow
from the Federal Home Loan Bank Board (FHLBB) (see Fig. 2.4).

Cost of Fixed-Rate Mortgages

This is the average cost of 30-year conventional loans on new homes (see
Fig. 2.5).

Obviously a borrower wants to pick an index which shows some stabil-

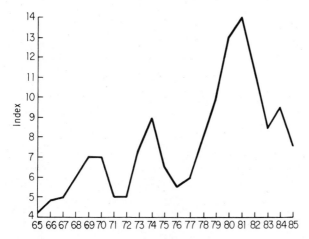

Figure 2.1. Six-month Treasury securities.

ity over time (see Fig. 2.6 for a comparison of two indices). But be careful. An index which is volatile when it is down, may give you a better beginning interest rate than an index which is stable but stays up.

This came home to many lenders and borrowers in 1985 and 1986. At that time one of the most stable indices had been the cost of funds for S&Ls. However, when interest rates in general began to drop in those years, this rate stayed high.

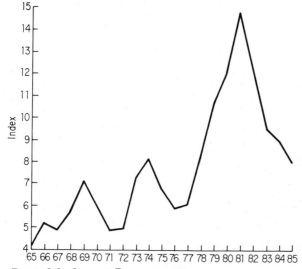

Figure 2.2. One-year Treasury securities.

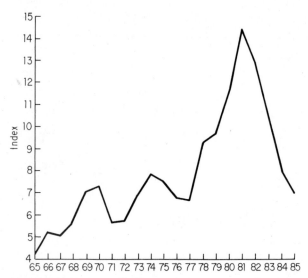

Figure 2.3. Three-year Treasury securities.

On the other hand, the Treasury rates plummeted. As a result, people with mortgages tied to the S&L rate continued to pay a high interest rate, while those holding mortgages tied to the Treasury yields saw their interest rates fall. Many lenders, seeing this happen, quickly switched indices on new ARMs they were issuing. (It is almost impossible to switch

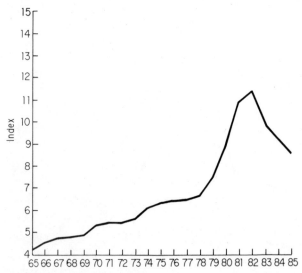

Figure 2.4. Cost of funds index.

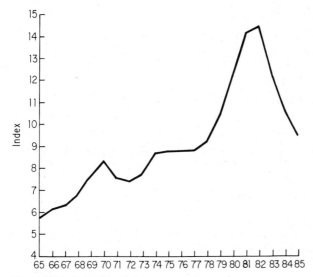

Figure 2.5. Cost of fixed-rate mortgages.

an index on an existing mortgage.) They were thus able to offer new lower-rate mortgages.

Of course, if interest rates rise in the future, the Treasury yields may be the first to go up and go up sharply. Hence those who got ARMs tied to Treasury yields during this period may live to regret it.

> *Rule 1: If you plan to keep the mortgage a long time, go for the index that is most stable. If you plan to keep the mortgage a short time, consider an index that is currently the lowest.*

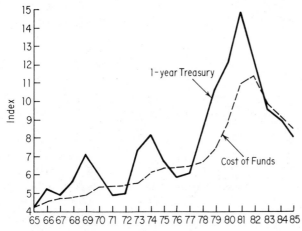

Figure 2.6. Comparison of two favorite indices—1-year Treasury and cost of funds.

Adjustment Period

After the index, the next critical feature to look for in an ARM is the adjustment period. How frequently can the lender adjust the mortgage rate up or down?

The adjustment period is arbitrary, and each lender will specify what it wants in the loan documents. Therefore, for the borrower this is a negotiable item. Most borrowers want *long* adjustment periods. Most lenders want *short* periods. Therefore, when we go shopping for a mortgage, it is highly advisable to place the adjustment period as a big priority on our list of terms to look for.

Typical Adjustment Periods

Lenders have become quite creative in their choice of adjustment periods. The most common are mortgages which are adjusted every month and mortgages which are adjusted every year. Next in popularity are mortgages which are adjusted every 6 months. Of course, there are some which adjust every 2 years or even every 3 years. Typically the adjustment period will be in some way linked to the "period" of the index. A mortgage which is adjusted every month will usually follow the shortest-term index, for example, the 6-month T-bill rate. One that is adjusted annually will typically follow the 1-year Treasury security or the cost-of-funds rate.

There are also many hybrid mortgages. Some offer a so-called "fixed rate" for the first year or two, then become adjustable. Others are adjustable for the first 7 years, then convert to a fixed rate. Some are even written for 30 years, but become all due and payable in 7 or 10 years. These latter are, in effect, short-term mortgages. The variations are endless.

What to Look For

In my opinion you want to look for *the longest adjustment period* you can get. This gives the greatest stability to the interest rate *and* to the monthly payment.

However, if you get a long adjustment period, in my opinion you should get it tied to a highly stable index, otherwise you could end up playing "catch-up."

What I mean by playing catch-up is this: Some ARMs specifically state that any interest not reflected in the current adjustment period will be carried forward to the next adjustment. Thus, today's upward movement in your index may cause future adjustments for years to come. This problem will be covered in greater detail in the next chapter, under the heading "Interest Rate Caps."

Rule 2: Go for the longest adjustment period you can get.

Convertibility

Some ARMs contain a special clause which will allow the borrower to *convert* to a fixed-rate mortgage at specified times in the future. Typically these times are at the end of each adjustment period after a certain number of years. If the borrower chooses to convert, the interest rate on the new fixed-rate mortgage is typically the then-current market interest rate.

Sometimes there are costs for converting. Frequently the lender will include 1 point (1 percent of the mortgage amount) or more as the conversion fee.

Watch out! Just because your mortgage contains a conversion clause does not automatically mean it is convertible. A friend of mine recently found this out the hard way.

Interest rates had declined sharply since he had obtained his ARM, and he decided it was an appropriate time to convert to a fixed-rate mortgage. His ARM contained a conversion clause. But he had not read it all the way through to the last sentence, which read: "This mortgage CAN [ ] CANNOT [ ] be converted." The lender had checked the "Cannot" box and refused to allow a conversion. Thus the borrower had to go through the expense of a costly refinance.

Conversions are great features to have and increase the advantages of the ARM. They are particularly useful, as noted above, when interest rates decline.

To Come

There are many other vital features of ARMs to be considered before anyone makes the decision to get one. We will cover these in the chapters that follow.

3

Caps: Do They Really Make ARMs Safer?

In the last chapter we looked at three important features of ARMs: the index, the adjustment period, and convertibility. There are, however, a number of other features that are of vital importance: one of the most sought after of these (by borrowers) is called a "cap."

Caps

This is the area that most borrowers immediately ask about. Are there "caps" on the ARM they are considering? (As we'll see, "caps" aren't nearly as important as borrowers think—there are other far more important items which borrowers frequently overlook.)

The term "caps" refers to limits placed on the interest rate or the monthly payment or both. Without caps on an ARM, there is potentially no limit to the interest rate or the monthly payment. With caps, both can rise (or fall) only so far.

Let's be sure we understand how a cap works. Let's say that our ARM has a 5 percent cap on the interest rate. That means that no matter what happens to the index, whether it goes up or down, our mortgage can never fluctuate more than 5 percent in either direction from its original rate.

For example, we take out a mortgage with a 10 percent interest rate and a 5 percent cap. What's the maximum and minimum interest rate this mortgage can have? Let's look at an example: a $100,000 mortgage with an original rate of 10 percent, a 5 percent cap, and a 30-year term.

		Monthly payment
Maximum interest rate	15%	$1264
Original interest rate	10%	878
Minimum interest rate	5%	492

For this borrower, the cap prevents the mortgage interest rate from rising above 15 percent. The maximum the payment could ever go to would be $1264. Without the cap, the interest rate would be unlimited and theoretically could go to 20 percent or higher.

Are Interest Rate Caps Beneficial?

Nearly all borrowers would agree that interest rate caps are beneficial. Yes, they would say, we want to be protected against runaway interest rates.

However, interest rate caps are deceptive. They don't really give as much protection as they seem to. For example, the historical high on interest rates in the last 50 years was roughly 17 percent, set during 1980 and 1981. It's unlikely that such high rates will appear again in the near future.

In the above example, the 5 percent cap would put the mortgage very close to that historical high. Thus the chances of the mortgage ever getting to its maximum interest rate are fairly low. (Don't get me wrong, it could happen, but it's just not likely.) What this means is that the chances are that, during the life of the loan, the interest rate will bounce around *within the 5 percent cap parameters*. Thus this cap may never come into play.

Many borrowers would pooh-pooh this, noting that the cap is there nonetheless in case catastrophe strikes. However, lenders are more realistic. They allow a 5 percent cap (in this case) precisely because they know it's unlikely it will ever be invoked. They give the borrower very little while taking a great deal of applause in the meantime.

A Better Way to Look at Caps

From the borrower's perspective (your perspective), it's not just the fact that a mortgage has an interest rate cap that is important. Rather it's the *size* of the cap that is vital.

Thus, a mortgage with a 3 percent cap is a far better mortgage than one with a 5 percent cap. And a mortgage with a 2 percent cap is better than the others. While this may seem obvious, it nevertheless is a consideration.

Rule 3: Get the lowest interest rate cap you can find.

Steps

We'll return to interest rate caps in a few pages, but for now let's consider something I feel is even more important to the borrower than mortgage rate caps, the "steps." (Unfortunately, few lenders impress the importance of the steps on the borrower.)

"Steps" refers to the amount by which the mortgage interest rate can be increased (or decreased) *each adjustment period.* You'll recall that we talked about adjustment periods in the last chapter. We noted that the mortgage interest rate could be adjusted periodically, typically anywhere from each month to every 3 years.

At the time of adjustment the interest rate is raised or lowered, depending on what the index has done. But by how much? Can it be raised, for example, to the interest rate cap? Let's say interest rates on our index have gone through the roof. Can our mortgage interest rate in one adjustment period be raised to its cap? If the original rate (as per our example) was 10 percent and the cap was 5 percent, can the interest rate be hiked upward to 15 percent in one adjustment period?

If the loan did not have steps, then the answer would be "Yes!" However, nearly all ARMs have steps, or limits on the hikes in interest rate per adjustment period. These limits are typically anywhere from ½ of a percent to 2½ percent per adjustment period. Thus, regardless of how the mortgage's index behaves, the interest rate cannot change more than the step amount each period.

The amount of the step can be more important than the cap on the interest rate!

Importance of Steps

Here are two different mortgages. The first has steps of 1 percent. The second has steps of 2 percent. Both mortgages have adjustment periods of 6 months. Notice what happens to the interest rate and payments with the two different steps (see Fig. 3.1).

The interest rate went from 10 to 14 percent over a period of time and

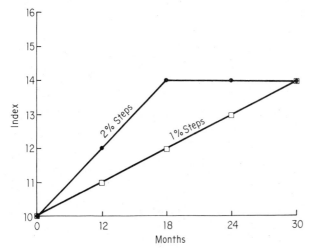

Figure 3.1. Mortgage steps—1 percent vs 2 percent steps

then started down. This is typically how interest rates behave. They don't go up and stay up or go down and stay down; they fluctuate.

Notice that the mortgage with the 2 percent steps followed the rate right up there and was at 14 percent within 6 months of the index. Notice also, however, that the mortgage with the 1 percent steps lagged behind. Because this mortgage could only be increased by 1 percent each adjustment period, it couldn't rise as quickly. Hence, by the time it finally got to 12 percent, the index was already turning down. The mortgage with the 1 percent steps takes longer to get to 14 percent.

The point to be taken here is that the smaller the steps, the greater the lag when there is a sudden jump in interest rates. (Of course, a sudden decline would not be felt as quickly, either.) If we assume that interest rates will tend to move both up and down, the smaller the steps, therefore, the more stable the mortgage. Small steps, in fact, can have a far greater impact on the stability of the mortgage than an interest rate cap.

Rule 4: The smaller the steps, the greater the stability of the mortgage.

Catch-up

In the early days of ARMs, many lenders were concerned about this very problem with steps. Naturally enough, they wanted the mortgage interest rate to keep pace with the index, and they quickly saw that mortgages with small steps would lag. Consequently, they often wrote "catch-up" clauses into mortgages. These clauses provided that even though the

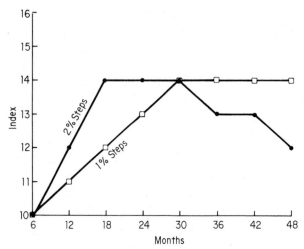

Figure 3.2. Mortgage steps—catch up. One percent steps play catch up with index.

mortgage interest rate didn't rise fast enough to keep pace with the index, any interest lost to the lender in this fashion *would be carried over to the next adjustment period.*

With a catch-up clause in a mortgage, the beneficial effects of smaller steps are nullified over a long period of time. In the previous example, the mortgage with 1 percent steps would continue to increase toward the maximum *even after the index had turned down* until all the interest due to increases in the rate had been given to the lender (see Fig. 3.2).

This catch-up effect proved to be extremely confusing to borrowers, who would find their interest rates and mortgage payments rising just when the index had turned and was beginning to fall. Borrower lawsuits and public complaints quickly convinced lenders that catch-up meant trouble.

Consequently, in recent years lenders have tended to reduce the number of catch-up clauses in mortgages. Today many ARMs writers, instead of using catch-ups, simply opt for bigger steps. Two percent steps are becoming increasingly common.

For the borrower, my advice is to shop for a lender who offers both lower steps and no catch-up clauses.

Rule 5: Avoid mortgages with catch-up clauses if at all possible.

Note: Although catch-up clauses tend to nullify the beneficial effect of smaller steps in the long run, they may not do so in the short run. If you plan to sell the property fairly quickly, small steps even with a catch-up clause can prove beneficial by offering lower payments.

Monthly Payment Caps

Thus far we've talked about caps to the interest rate. If you're new to mortgages and you've read this far, you've surely come to the conclusion that the whole process is, if nothing else, complex. Many readers, I am sure, are asking themselves, "Why can't it be made simpler?"

In response to this some lenders offer something which on the surface does appear to be simpler. They cap the monthly payment. (This can be done in conjunction with an interest rate cap or independent of it with strikingly different results, as we'll soon see.)

A monthly payment cap states that the payment cannot rise by more than a certain percentage of the previous period's payment. The most common payment cap is 7.5 percent. The payment in the new adjustment period cannot increase by more than 7.5 percent of the payment for the preceding period.

Effect of a Monthly Payment Cap of 7.5 Percent
on a 30-Year, $100,000 Mortgage

	Previous period	New period
Interest rate	10%	12%
Payment without monthly cap	$878	$1029
Payment with 7.5% cap	$878	$ 944
Difference		$ 85

When interest rates rise dramatically, the monthly payment cap keeps the payment relatively stable. In the above example the payment cap kept the payment from rising by an additional $85.

Beware of Simple Solutions

Borrowers who are scrimping to make the monthly payment and who are terrified of payment increases often jump at the chance to get a monthly payment cap. They feel that in so doing they are taking a major step in protecting themselves.

There are three reasons why I think they are wrong. The first is that capping the monthly payment frequently results in "negative amortization." The $85 a month saved in our previous example is simply added to the mortgage balance. Thus the mortgage actually increases over time! (We'll have a lot more to say about this in the next chapter.)

The second reason I don't like monthly caps is that they are a trade-off for other more important benefits. A lender who offers a monthly pay-

Table 3.1. Effects of Monthly Payment Caps on Size of Monthly Payment over the Life of the Loan
$50,000, 30-Year Mortgage.

Year	Interest rate, %	Monthly payment			
		7% cap	7.5% cap	10% cap	No cap
1	12	$514	$514	$514	$514
2	13.5	540	552	565	572
3	15	567	594	622	630
4	16.5	595	638	684	689
5	18	625	686	753	748
6	18	656	738	753	748
10	18	797	800	753	748
15	18	1018	800	753	748
20	18	1112	800	753	748
25	18	1112	800	753	748
29	18	1112	800	753	748

ment cap as an inducement to a borrower often feels justified in asking for more restrictive terms in other areas. For example, such a lender may want bigger steps. The borrower may give up the vital benefit of small steps for the apparent benefit of a monthly payment cap. It's sort of like the Indians who sold Manhattan for $24 worth of beads.

Third, the ultimate monthly payment with a cap may be higher than without. Consider Table 3.1, prepared by the Federal Home Loan Bank Board, which shows the effect of various monthly payment caps on the monthly payment over a period of 29 years. The example assumes that interest rates start at 12 percent, then rise to 18 percent at year 5 and remain there. It also assumes that there is no interest rate cap on the $50,000 mortgage.

Notice that the lower the monthly payment cap, the lower the monthly payments *initially*. But over the long run, the lower the monthly payment cap, *the higher the monthly payments*. A 7.5 percent cap (the most commonly used today), for example, will result after year 10, in this case, in a payment of $800. Without the cap the payment would only have been $748.

> *Rule 6. Monthly payment caps can mean lower monthly payments now, but higher monthly payments later on.*

Monthly Payment Cap *with* an Interest Rate Cap

The above example was exaggerated to make a point. (No one expects interest rates to move to 18 percent and stay there.) Also, one important consideration was left out: A mortgage might have *both* a monthly payment cap *and* an interest rate cap.

Some lenders use this combination, and borrowers sometimes think that it is a significantly better loan. The loan with the interest rate capped is indeed better for the borrower. But it is questionable if there is a significant benefit when a monthly payment cap is also included.

To see why, look back at our previous example. Let's say that in addition to the monthly payment being capped, the interest rate was capped at a 6 percent maximum change with steps of 1½ percent per year. *The chart would work out exactly the same!* The interest rate cap would have no effect since the interest rate only rose to the maximum (from 12 percent in our example to 18 percent) and the increases were never more than 1½ percent a year.

Only if the interest rate cap were lower (in our example, less than 6 percent), would it act to mitigate the negative effects of a monthly payment cap. For example, a 5 percent interest rate cap would prevent the interest rate from rising above 17 percent in the above example. This would reduce the total negative interest under the monthly payment cap.

Hint: When a mortgage has both an interest rate cap and a monthly payment cap, you automatically should know that the interest rate cap is set higher than the monthly payment cap and that negative amortization could take place. The reason is simple: If this weren't the case, if the interest rate cap were set sufficiently low that no negative amortization could take place, then no monthly payment cap would be necessary.

> *Rule 7: Avoid monthly payment caps—look instead for lower interest rate caps, longer adjustment periods, and lower steps.*

The Bottom Line

We've looked into the problems and advantages of capping mortgages and having smaller steps. In the next chapter we'll examine even more features of concern.

4

Three Hidden Problems with ARMs

We've seen what an ARM (adjustable-rate mortgage) is and how it works. We might have the impression that once it's explained it's fairly straight-forward. However, hidden from view are three distinct problems that can occur with ARMs that could ultimately lead to the most dreaded of real estate consequences: foreclosure.

In this chapter we're going to look into these three hidden and often misunderstood problems. The goal here is to unveil what's really happening so that you can avoid making what could be a dreadful mistake when you finance property.

Problem 1—The Hidden Discount

Because it is so little understood, this is probably the area that causes the greatest problems for borrowers carrying ARMs today. Many borrowers simply are unaware that their ARM has been discounted and do not see the dire consequences this could have for them.

The reason for this is easy to understand. Discounting is little mentioned in loan documents. These documents usually shout about the APR (annual percentage rate), but whisper about discounting. You have to know where to read and what to look for to find mention of it.

The hidden discount comes as close to being a ripoff of the borrower as anything I've seen in the mortgage field today. However, I have yet to see any consumer advocate blow the whistle on it.

The Margin

To see the problem with discounting we first have to understand the "margin." The margin is an additional amount that the lender *adds* to the index rate each time the loan rate is adjusted.

For example, let's say that our ARM is tied to the 1-year T-bill rate. That rate for the current adjustment period happens to be 8 percent. Does that mean that our mortgage interest rate will also be 8 percent?

In almost all cases the answer is *"No,"* our mortgage rate will be higher. The lender *adds* usually anywhere from 1 to 3 percent to the index to get our mortgage rate. Let's say the lender adds 2 percent.

Adding the Margin to the Index
to Find the Mortgage Rate

Index	8%
Margin	2%
Mortgage rate	10%

Why Lenders Add Margins

Lenders say they add a margin to cover their cost of business. This is only partly true. The other part that they don't explain is that the margin is added to bring the mortgage interest rate in line with the general market for mortgage rates. Thus if the T-bill rate is 8 percent and the overall mortgage market interest rate is 11 percent, they are inclined to make their margin 3 percent.

Of course, this only brings it in line at the time the mortgage is issued. As time goes by the difference between the margin selected and the market rate for mortgages may grow wider or narrower. The lender likes it when the spread grows narrower, and dislikes it, naturally enough, when the spread grows wide. Thus lenders, to protect themselves, usually insist on as high a margin as possible.

The Introductory Discount

Now that we understand the margin, we're ready to tackle the discount. The best way of understanding discounting is to take an example:

Interest Rate for a Typical ARM

Current index rate	10%
Margin	+2%
Correct interest rate	12%

The correct interest rate for the above ARM would be 12 percent. However, that also happens to be the current market for fixed-rate mortgages. But who in their right mind would get an ARM when a fixed-rate mortgage is available at the same interest rate?

Probably no one. Thus, to induce borrowers to go with their ARM, lenders offer an "introductory discount." When we ask how much the ARM's interest rate is, we are not given the correct rate, 12 percent, but instead are given the introductory discounted rate. If the introductory discount happens to be 3 percent, we are told the ARM is only 9 percent! What's more, to get the mortgage we only have to qualify at 9 percent instead of at 12.

Needless to say, we are attracted. The ARM appears to be 3 full points below the fixed-rate mortgage market, a real bargain.

The Problem

Thus far everything is "kosher." However, if we are the typical borrower, we now make a few understandable assumptions. These assumptions are incorrect, but I have yet to find a lender that will go out of its way to point this fact out.

False Assumption 1

If our index goes down by 1 or 2 percent by the next adjustment period, our mortgage interest rate will go down.

Why is this false? Isn't the mortgage interest rate linked to the index? If the index goes down, doesn't the mortgage interest rate have to go down?

Normally the answer would be yes. However, we have received an introductory discount. The 9 percent we are paying is currently 3 percent below the true and correct interest rate we should be paying.

If the index goes down by 1 percent, we will still be 2 percent below the correct rate. If the index goes down 2 percent, we'll still be 1 percent below the correct rate. The index, in this example, must go down 3 full percentage points for our mortgage interest rate to remain the same.

Interest Rate vs. Index

Index rate, %	Margin, %	Correct mortgage rate, %	Our rate, %	Difference, %
10	2	12	9	3
9	2	11	9	2
8	2	10	9	1
7	2	9	9	0

What the chart shows us is that the index rate must fall *more* than 3 percent *before* our mortgage interest rate will drop.

False Assumption 2

If our index remains at the same rate, our mortgage interest rate will remain the same.

The reason this is false is because the discount is only *introductory*. It only lasts until the end of the first adjustment period. *If* the index remains constant *and* our mortgage is adjusted every 6 months *and* there is no cap on the adjustment, then at the next adjustment period our mortgage interest rate will jump from 9 percent to 12 percent.

Of course, if the adjustment period is longer or if there is a cap, the jump may be less steep and take longer. For example, *if* the index remains constant *and* our mortgage is adjusted annually with a maximum step of 1½ percent per adjustment, then it will take 2 years for our mortgage interest rate to get from 9 percent to 12 percent.

The idea to keep sight of in all this, however, is that because the discount is *introductory,* if the index remains constant, then our mortgage interest rate *must* go up.

False Assumption 3

Our payment will not go up unless the index goes up.

If you've read this far, by now you should see why this is incorrect. Assuming we don't have a monthly payment cap, the only way the payments will not go up is if the index goes down. In our example the index would have to drop by 3 points so that the correct interest rate would equal the mortgage rate we are paying to prevent an increase of payments at the beginning of the next adjustment period. If the index remains constant or only goes down slightly, our monthly payments *must* rise.

Why It's a Real Problem

By now you probably see the problem with the introductory discount. Borrowers are lured to the ARM by a low initial interest rate. Many never really understand that the low rate applies only until the next adjustment period and that unless the index goes down, the rate will automatically go up each adjustment period until it reaches the correct interest rate.

For the person who is struggling to qualify, who has trouble just making the monthly payments at the introductory rate, this can be a devastating problem. In some cases it has caused buyers to default and to lose their property to foreclosure. In many other cases it has produced extreme and unexpected financial and emotional strain on the borrowers.

Why Isn't Something Done to Protect the Borrower?

Many lenders continue to discount ARMs for a simple reason. They are basically a less desirable mortgage for the borrower in most cases, and without the discount, no one would want them. The lender discounts the ARM to get borrowers to take it.

Additionally, all the information we've just been discussing is normally contained in the loan documents. The index is specified, the margin is indicated, and the initial interest rate is stated. The only thing that is frequently left out is a clear explanation of the consequences of taking an introductory discount. One lender who I talked with and who asks to remain anonymous said, "If the borrower wants to make false assumptions about the loan, that's his problem. All the borrower has to do is ask, and we'll clearly confirm that the monthly payment and the interest rate will rise if the index doesn't change."

In other words, *caveat emptor*. "Let the buyer (or in this case the borrower) beware." The lender will indeed confirm and probably explain, *if* you know the right questions to ask.

What You Should Do to Avoid the Problem

Now that you understand it, look for it. Ask this question of the lender or the person who takes your loan application when you are getting an ARM: *"If the index remains constant, what will happen to the mortgage interest rate and my payment at the next adjustment period?"*

If the person says that it will *not* go up, get them to put that in writing and to sign it. (Later, if it turns out they were wrong, the lender could be liable for damages up to three times the value of the mortgage!)

If the answer is that it will go up, then ask: *"If the index remains constant, what will be my exact mortgage payment at the next two adjustment periods?"*

This should give you a pretty good idea of what to expect in terms of monthly payments.

A True Story

I recently was asked for some advice on a mortgage by a young couple buying their first home. It was in the San Francisco Bay area where prices are relatively high. They could just barely afford the down payment on the house, and they would be struggling to make the monthly payments. The only mortgage they could qualify for was an ARM with an introductory discount of 2 percent.

Their initial payments would be $1400 a month. With both of them working, they figured they could just squeak by at this. They asked if I thought they should go ahead with the loan and the mortgage.

I asked them how long the adjustment periods were and what the maximum adjustment was per period (the steps). Six months and 2 percent, they told me. My next question to them was, "Can you afford payments of about $1700 a month right now?" No, they answered, they certainly couldn't.

I suggested they forget the mortgage and either find some other way of financing the property or forget the property as well. They were shocked. Why should I insist they were facing $1700 payments right away. "Our payments will only be $1400 a month. We can worry about what happens if they go up in the future, when they go up."

I asked them if they expected interest rates in general to plummet in the next 6 months. They said they didn't know. To which I responded that if we assumed that interest rates remained constant, then the seventh monthly payment they had to make (at the start of the next adjustment period) would be close to $1700, *automatically*.

"But that's in the future," they protested.

Six months? That's like tomorrow, I replied. Did they know that their income would increase by that much in such a short period of time. If not, how would the make the higher payments?

We were at a stalemate. They wanted the house, but they didn't want to hear what I was telling them. They went away, and I suspected that they were going to buy the property anyhow. (I later learned that they didn't. Instead they found a cheaper house they could better afford.)

The Moral

Don't be like the fish who gives up its life for a juicy-looking little worm. With mortgages the first adjustment period can pass like a flash, and then you could be up against the correct and true interest rate. Better to face it now, before you get the loan, than later when you're already on the hook.

Note: As mentioned in the last chapter, some shrewd borrowers who plan to resell quickly will go one up on the mortgage company. They will take advantage of the introductory discount and then sell when the rate goes up.

Remember, there is nothing wrong with getting an ARM with an introductory discount, *as long as the borrower fully understands what's happening and agrees to it.* The problem is that many borrowers are simply unaware that the ARM they are acquiring has been discounted.

Problem 2—Underqualifying

This problem follows from problem number 1 above. In the early 1980s underqualifying was a severe problem and led to numerous foreclosures by 1985. By 1986, however, regulators had clamped down on lenders so that the most grievious instances no longer occurred. Nevertheless, the borrower must be aware that this problem can always crop up.

Why Qualifying Is Important

Almost any time we get a mortgage, we must "qualify" for it. This means that we must demonstrate our ability to repay.

As we've already seen, besides a good credit history and sufficient down payment, this also means that we have enough income to make the monthly payments. If we can't make the payments, ultimately we will lose the property one way or another.

Qualifying and the ARM

In the past, borrowers were qualified for an ARM *not* on the true and correct market rate of the mortgage (as explained above) but rather on the basis of the introductory discount rate. The result was an underqualified borrower who frequently got into trouble as soon as the mortgage rate went up. Here's how it happened:

Qualifying at the Introductory Discount Rate
(True Market Rate—11%)

Mortgage amount	$100,000
Starting interest rate	9%
Monthly payment (30-year term)	$ 804
Monthly income needed to qualify for loan	$ 2412

The monthly payment on the mortgage is roughly $800. To qualify (assuming income must be three times monthly payment and for the moment forgetting about taxes and insurance), the lender determines that the borrower should be making at least $2412. With this income the borrower, in theory, should be able to afford the payments.

The Making of a Problem

However, without the introductory discount, the true and correct interest rate on the mortgage is 11 percent instead of 9 percent.

Qualifying at the True and Correct
Mortgage Rate

Mortgage amount	$100,000
Fixed interest rate	11%
Monthly payment (30-year term)	$ 952
Monthly income needed to qualify	$ 2856

At the true and correct rate, the borrower should be making $2856 to qualify for this loan. The difference can be critical.

Qualifying at Correct Rate vs. Qualifying at
Introductory Discount

	Mortgage amount	Payment	Needed to qualify
Correct	$100,000	$952	$2856
Discounted	100,000	804	2412
Difference:			$ 444

The difference of $444 a month is the additional income the borrower should have to qualify at the true and correct mortgage rate. If the borrower doesn't make this much money, then when the rate is adjusted upward (as explained under "Problem 1"), he or she may not be able to afford the new payment.

The Problem

If the borrower would have qualified at 11 percent (was making $2856 a month instead of $2412), there shouldn't be any problem. But at the lower monthly income, the payment suddenly becomes almost 40 percent of the borrower's total income, a staggering and in many cases unmanageable burden.

The problem comes about when lenders get too greedy in their desire to "get the money loaned out" and borrowers are too shortsighted (or underinformed) to make a good judgment in terms of qualifying.

How to Avoid the Problem

The way to avoid this problem is easy. *If the lender won't qualify you at the true and correct interest rate, do it yourself!*

Find out what the true and correct payments should be and then determine if you can indeed afford them. (I always add 5 percent to the payments, just to be safe.) If you can still afford them, then go ahead. But if realistically you can't, don't get the ARM even if the lender says you qualify.

Remember, unless you have a game plan ready for when the payments jump up (such as refinancing or selling), you could be in for real "payment shock"!

Problem 3—Negative Amortization

Today negative amortization occurs in a substantial number of ARMs. It is not something which is hidden from the borrower. Typically the negative amortization terms are fully explained in those mortgages in which it occurs. Yet, for some reason, many borrowers still fail to see the drawbacks.

Negative amortization means that instead of the mortgage balance going down, it goes up! Each month, instead of paying off some of the loan, we add to it. We end up owing *more* than we originally borrowed and, what I feel is even worse, we end up paying interest on interest.

The Cause of Negative Amortization

Negative amortization typically comes about because borrowers are desperate to control their monthly payment. For these borrowers the principal concern is that the monthly payment not rise too swiftly. Typically such borrowers have limited ability to increase their income. They are afraid that sudden large monthly payment increases could cause them to lose their property. They are seeking protection.

This borrower, therefore, is highly susceptible to the lender who offers to "cap" the monthly payment. Under such a cap the monthly payment will not be allowed to rise beyond a set amount regardless of what the interest rate does. For example, the most common monthly payment cap is 7.5 percent. If our monthly payment is $1000 and we have such a cap, at the next adjustment period the payment cannot rise by more than 7.5 percent, or to a maximum of $1075.

However, a monthly payment cap alone *does not limit interest rate increases.* What a monthly payment cap does is to restrict that portion of the interest rate increase that the borrower immediately pays. The portion that the borrower does not pay, however, does not go away. Rather, it is added to the mortgage. Consider the following example:

What Happens When the Monthly
Payment Is Not Capped

	Original	After interest rate increase
Mortgage amount	$100,000	$100,000
Interest rate	10%	12%
Monthly payment	$ 878	$ 1028

In the example above, the interest rate has risen from 10 percent to 12 percent on an ARM. The monthly payment to fully pay off the mortgage should rise from $878 a month to $1028. But let's assume this mortgage has a monthly payment cap. The most commonly used cap today states that the monthly payment "will not be allowed to rise by more than 7.5 percent from the previous adjustment period."

Table 4.1. Effect of Capping Monthly Payment on 30-Year, $50,000 Mortgage with an Initial Interest Rate of 12 Percent*

Year	Rate, %	Monthly payment		Remaining balance	
		5% cap	7.5% cap	5% cap	7.5% cap
1	12	$514	$514	$49,818	$49,818
2	13.5	540	552	50,079	49,915
3	15	567	594	50,837	50,295
4	16.5	595	638	52,180	50,977
5	18	625	686	54,236	51,992
6	18	656	738	56,284	52,534

*Information for this table supplied by the Federal Home Loan Bank Board.

Previous monthly payment	$878
Increase allowed	×0.075
Increase in payment	66
New monthly payment	$944

The maximum new payment allowed is $944. However, the mortgage calls for a payment of $1028. There is a discrepancy of $84 per month.

Correct monthly payment	$1028
Maximum allowed payment	−944
Difference	$ 84

What happens to that $84? Is it forgiven? Not on your life. It is added to the mortgage amount (principal) still owed. Next month this borrower will owe $84 more than he or she owed this month. Next month this borrower will pay interest not only on the original amount borrowed, but also on this extra $84. That is paying interest on interest.

But what's $84? Isn't it a negligible amount? Hardly. Over a period of years it can add up to a staggering amount. Consider Table 4.1.

In the above example the remaining balance on the mortgage will increase by $6466 over 6 years with a 5 percent monthly cap, and by $2716 with a 7.5 percent monthly cap. The reason the increase is so dramatic is that the borrower is paying interest on interest.

(*Note:* The above example uses only a $50,000 mortgage. Double the effects for a $100,000 mortgage, and triple them for a $150,000 mortgage.)

Will Appreciation Offset Negative Amortization?

Often an argument used by lenders to justify the bad effects of negative amortization is that housing price increases will more than offset it. Yes, we might be adding to the mortgage amount, but our house will be worth more anyhow, so why worry?

This argument is fallacious. Housing prices do *not* always go up. In most parts of the country, for example, they declined between 1981 and 1984. In the farm belt in the midwest, they declined so dramatically between 1981 and 1986 that in some cases negative amortization could have contributed to a borrower owing more on the mortgage than the property was worth!

Additionally, from the borrower's perspective, price increases in property have traditionally been a way of increasing equity. In fact, one of the principal reasons for buying real estate has always been to take advantage of the profit potential in price increases.

With negative amortization, however, the mortgage increase eats into that equity, into the potential profit. With negative amortization the lender, in effect, shares some of the increase.

Opinion

To my way of thinking this is grossly unfair. The lender gets its reward by charging interest on the mortgage. The borrower/buyer, on the other hand, is entitled to the reward of equity increase for the risks of ownership. For the lender to share some of the borrower's reward is "double dipping." It's getting paid twice for the same risk.

Additionally, from an historical perspective, charging interest on interest has always been taboo. There are Biblical covenants against it. During the Middle Ages in Europe any merchant found guilty of charging interest on interest faced immediate ostracization from the community, if not more severe punishment. To me it is one of the contradictions of our civilization that in our supposedly enlightened age regulating authorities not only condone negative amortization, but in some cases encourage it!

How to Avoid Negative Amortization

The great tragedy here is that negative amortization really isn't necessary. If you want to control the monthly payment on your mortgage, you can best accomplish your goal by shopping around for an ARM that has small adjustment steps.

A mortgage with steps for each adjustment period of not more than 1 percent will actually provide smaller monthly payment increases per ad-

justment period than a similar mortgage with higher steps and a monthly payment cap of 7.5 percent.

Think about it. With just a little bit of shopping around, you could avoid the negative amortization trap.

The Bottom Line

We've looked at three separate problems commonly encountered by borrowers who take out ARMs. My suggestion is that if an ARM is in your future, you put a little marker in this chapter. Come back here just before you sign the documents to make sure you're not making a mistake.

5
ARMs: Quick Definitions and Comparison Chart

If you want to quickly figure out what an ARM is and how it works, this chapter should help. The definitions are short and to the point. The comparison chart at the end of the chapter should be extremely helpful in shopping for the best ARM available.

Definitions

Index

The interest rate on nearly all ARMs is tied to an index. As the index moves up, the interest rate on the ARM goes up. As the index goes down, so does the interest rate on the ARM. See Chapter 2 for the various indices which may be used.

Margin

Lenders add 1 or more percentage points to the index to arrive at the interest rate for the ARM. This "margin" does not usually change for the life of the loan. One reason the margin is added is to bring the index up to the current mortgage market rate. It is normally to the borrower's advantage to seek the smallest margin.

Index rate + margin = ARM interest rate

Adjustment Period

The "adjustment period" is the amount of time that must pass before the interest rate and/or the monthly payment can be changed by the lender. These periods vary from monthly to once every three or more years. It is usually to the borrower's advantage to get the *longest* adjustment period.

Caps

"Caps" are limits placed on the amount the lender can increase (or decrease) the interest rate for the life of the mortgage. In recent years the interest rate cap has typically been anywhere from 3 to 6 percent. It is often to the borrower's advantage to get the smallest cap possible.

The term "caps" also refers to the limit on the monthly payment increase (or decrease) regardless of what the interest rate does. This cap frequently works to the borrower's disadvantage by causing "negative amortization."

Steps

"Steps" are limits (or caps) on the amount that the lender can increase (or decrease) the interest rate *per adjustment period*. For example, the loan may have an overall interest rate cap of 5 percent, but the change in interest rate might be limited to steps of 2 percent *per adjustment period*. (The interest rate cannot be raised or lowered by more than 2 percent per period.) Steps offer greater protection against sharp monthly payment increases for the borrower. It is usually to the borrower's advantage in a rising interest rate market to get the smallest steps possible.

Introductory Discount

To induce borrowers to get ARMs, most lenders offer an introductory discount on the interest rate. This is normally a *one time* discount, which recently has been anywhere from 1 to 3 percent. In a stable interest rate market, the interest rate on an ARM usually rises each adjustment period after the introductory discount until the advantage disappears. This can be a trap for the unwary borrower (see Chapter 4).

Introductory Rate Qualifying

This occurs when a lender qualifies a buyer on the basis of the introductory discount interest rate instead of the true and correct market rate. If the discount was steep and the interest rate market does not move downward, the monthly payments will increase, often to the point where the borrower cannot meet them. Borrowers should be wary of optimistic qualifying and should be sure they can meet the monthly payments that may realistically be assessed on the ARM after a few adjustment periods.

Negative Amortization

Negative amortization occurs when the interest due on the mortgage is not immediately paid but instead is added to principal. It results in the borrower owing more than was originally borrowed and paying interest on interest. It occurs when there is a cap on the monthly payment but no corresponding cap on the interest rate.

Payment Shock

Payment shock occurs when the monthly payment rises more steeply than the borrower expects at the beginning of an adjustment period. For example, if the payment was $800 a month and it suddenly moved to $1050, payment shock might occur for the borrower.

Payment shock can be reduced by capping the overall mortgage interest rate and having small steps in the adjustment period increases.

ARM Comparison Chart

	Mortgage 1	Mortgage 2	Mortgage 3
True interest rate	_____	_____	_____
Discounted rate	_____	_____	_____
How long will discount last?	_____	_____	_____
Index used	_____	_____	_____
Margin	_____	_____	_____
Adjustment period	_____	_____	_____
Interest rate cap	_____	_____	_____
Steps	_____	_____	_____
Monthly payment cap	_____	_____	_____
Negative amortization	_____	_____	_____
Years to pay off	_____	_____	_____
Convertibility	_____	_____	_____

Monthly Payment

What will the monthly payment be after 1 year if the index:

1. Goes up 2%?   _____   _____   _____

2. Stays the same?   _____   _____   _____

3. Goes down 2%?   _____   _____   _____

What will the monthly payment be after 3 years if the index:

1. Goes up 2% a year?   _____   _____   _____

2. Stays the same?   _____   _____   _____

3. Goes down 2% a year?   _____   _____   _____

6
Mortgage Features to Look For

There are certain features of every mortgage (ARM or fixed) that benefit us, the borrower. In this chapter we're going to cover three specific features: assumability, prepayment, and points.

Assumability

There's an old rule in real estate that goes something like this: The time to prepare your house for resale is *before* you buy it. People would have a lot easier time reselling if they paid more attention at the time they buy.

With regard to mortgages, the issue is assumability. This means that a new buyer can take over or "assume" an existing mortgage. To understand the advantage, let's take an example. We buy a home at a time when interest rates are low. We get a 10 percent *assumable* mortgage.

Five years later we want to sell. Interest rates are now at 15 percent. If a buyer who wanted to purchase our home had to get a new mortgage, he or she would be facing an enormous interest rate.

On the other hand, because our current loan is *assumable*, that buyer can take it over and get the benefit of our low 10 percent rate. (In this case it would mean a third less in monthly payments for the buyer.)

Having a good (low interest rate) assumable loan on a property is a definite plus when it's time to sell. Often a seller with an assumable can *ask a higher price and get it* because of the favorable terms. Almost always a good assumable loan ensures a faster sale. (*Note:* The buyer need not always pay cash down to the assumable loan. In most cases a second mortgage can be arranged for a portion of the purchase—check with your broker or attorney.)

Due-on-Sale Clauses

Any mortgage can be assumable. Most, however, are not. Most mortgages contain a "due-on-sale clause." This means that when we sell the property the mortgage is "accelerated" or becomes all due and payable. In effect, we must pay it off—the new buyer cannot take it over.

In the mid-1970s there were serious challenges to the due-on-sale clause contained in many mortgages. First, using "contracts of sale" (a selling instrument), many sellers were able to circumvent the due-on-sale clause. Later, lower courts ruled the clause invalid. For a time virtually all mortgages were considered assumable.

By the 1980s, however, higher courts had ruled that the due-on-sale clause was valid, and that is generally the position that holds sway as of this writing. If your mortgage contains a due-on-sale clause, chances are it's not assumable (although you may want to check with your attorney to be sure).

Why Lenders Don't Like Assumables

Lenders dislike assumable loans for a variety of reasons. The strongest reason is that such a loan transfers control from the lender to the borrower. Instead of the lender being able to determine who owes the money, the borrower can do it (by having someone assume the loan).

Lenders also fear getting stuck with low interest rate loans in a high interest rate market. In the early 1980s many lenders nearly went bankrupt because they held portfolios of loans in the 9 percent range while the mortgage market interest rate was above 15 percent. The way they bailed out of this was through nonassumability. When the borrower resold the property, he or she had to pay off the old low interest rate loan and get a new one. (*Note:* As those in real estate know, it is not necessary to get the new loan from the old lender. Any lender will do.)

Finding Assumable Loans Today

As a negotiating point, any lender can make any mortgage assumable. In residential real estate, however, there is little to no negotiation on this point. If we want the loan, we have to accept the due-on-sale clause.

There are, however, notable exceptions. Government-insured or -guaranteed loans (FHA and VA loans) are fully assumable. No due-on-sale clause can be written into them (as of this writing). That means that if we have such a mortgage, we can have *anyone* take it over. The new borrower *does not even need to qualify!* All that's required is to send a request to the lender (which the lender *must* honor) and to pay an assumption fee, usually around $50. However, beginning December 31, 1986, the FHA required lenders to obtain a good credit report from the buyer before allowing assumption of an FHA loan. (Similar restrictions may apply to. VA loans.)

Another source of assumables are ARMs. Many ARMs today include an assumability feature. There are usually, however, restrictions. The new borrower may take over the existing mortgage providing he or she *qualifies* and pays an assumption fee, typically 1 percent of the outstanding loan balance.

The assumability feature on an ARM is not that much of a plus since ARMs frequently are at (or sometimes above) market interest rate for mortgages.

Negotiating Assumability

Just because a mortgage has a due-on-sale clause does not automatically mean the lender will execute it. Sometimes lenders are willing to allow an assumption. With institutional mortgages (those from S&Ls, banks, etc.) the reason may be that the mortgage interest rate is close to the current market and the lender is dissatisfied with the way the current borrower has been making the payments. For example, if we're always 5 months late on our payment and the lender is always having to threaten foreclosure, then it might welcome a new borrower, *if* that borrower were better qualified and *if* that mortgage's interest rate were near market rate.

Additionally, if we hold a private mortgage, one given to us by a seller or a private individual, that person may be very willing to allow an assumption. Perhaps we'd need offer a couple of points to sweeten the pot or perhaps raise the interest rate a percentage point or two or even extend the loan or pay off a portion of it.

The point is that it doesn't hurt to ask. *Call the lender.* Ask the lender if it will allow an assumption. If the answer is no, ask if there is anything that will change the lender's mind (see the paragraph above). If the answer is still no, well, you've only wasted a phone call. But if the answer is yes . . . But get it in writing before starting a sale.

Prepayment

Some mortgages allow prepayment: that is, they allow the borrower to pay off the mortgage in advance. This is a vital feature to look for.

Say we had bought a home 7 years ago, and now we wanted to resell. However, our mortgage contained a clause against prepayment. Now, unless the lender were willing to let the new buyer assume the mortgage (something, as we've seen, which is unlikely), we couldn't sell!

Of course in actual practice prepayment clauses do not prevent us from selling. Instead they institute a penalty for early payment of the mortgage. Yes, we can resell *if* we pay the lender a penalty of perhaps 1 or 2 percent of the outstanding balance on the mortgage.

From the borrower's perspective, a prepayment penalty is a definite disadvantage.

Which Mortgages Have Prepayment Penalties?

Most older conventional (nongovernment) mortgages contain prepayment penalties. Typically that penalty reads something to the effect that if we prepay more than 20 percent of the outstanding balance at any one time, we will face a penalty equal to 6 months' interest.

For the last few years, however, most mortgages have not contained a prepayment penalty. The reason has to do with a point of law. A mortgage which contains *both* a prepayment penalty *and* a due-on-sale clause has in some courts been deemed unfairly restrictive. Hence, the lender is given a choice of one clause or the other. Typically lenders have opted for the due-on-sale clause and done away with the prepayment clause.

FHA and VA loans do not contain prepayment penalties. Most conventional, ARM as well as fixed rate, loans recently issued also do not contain penalties for prepayment.

However, some ARMs do contain restrictions on prepayment. They may, for example, require that to avoid the penalty the ARM must be paid off on or near the date of an adjustment. Be sure to check your ARM documents *before* you consider prepaying.

Points

Everyone in real estate uses points. However, there is some confusion about what they are.

In most cases a point is simply 1 percent of the amount of a mortgage. If our mortgage is $100,000, then 1 point would be $1000, 2 points would be $2000, 3 points would be $3000, and so forth.

When we obtain a mortgage, a lender typically charges us points. This is an additional fee paid up front when the mortgage is issued.

Buydowns

The lenders use points in a variety of ways. One way is to pay for the mortgage money between the time it is received from a previous lender who paid off a loan and a new lender who obtains a new loan. (Yes, lenders do try to cover all the bases!)

Another use of points is as a substitute for interest. By a complex calculation each point received at the time the mortgage is obtained can be shown to be roughly equivalent to a certain portion of the interest rate charge over the life of the mortgage. The calculation involves such things as future value of money and estimates of how long the mortgage will be in place before it is paid off. A rule of thumb is that 1 point equals ¼ to ½ a percent in interest.

Sometimes we can pay additional points to get a lower interest rate. For example, the market rate may be 10 percent. However, if we pay, for example, 3 points, the lender may be willing to give us a mortgage with a 9 percent interest rate. The points have substituted for the interest.

Builders frequently buy down mortgages on their houses in order to offer financing at very low interest rates. (Typically the rates are low only for the first few years of the mortgage—then they rise, often to higher than market levels.) Home sellers can also negotiate with lenders to buy down a mortgage interest rate in order to make the deal more appealing to a buyer.

Other Kinds of Points

Unfortunately, the term "points" is also used rather loosely in the business to mean other things. Another way "points" can be used is to divide 1 percent of interest into 100 parts. For example, ARMs typically have margins that might be equal to 2 or 3 percent of interest. However, these margins are not described as 2 or 3 percent of interest. They are described as 200 or 300 points. A typical margin, therefore, may be 200 points.

When dealing with points, therefore, it's important to ask, "Points of what?" If it's mortgage points, then we know each point equals 1 percent of the mortgage amount. If it's interest points, then we know that each point usually equals 1/100 of a percent of interest.

7
When to Refinance

Over the last 10 years, interest rates on home mortgages have fluctuated wildly. They have been as high as 17 percent and as low as 9 percent. Mortgages themselves have gone through a transition so that now we have a mixed market, with both fixed-rate mortgages and ARMs.

A borrower facing this hodgepodge is frequently forced to take a mortgage that he or she really doesn't want. Perhaps it's an ARM and the borrower wants fixed rate. Perhaps the interest rate is too high. Eventually times change, rates drop, and the borrower thinks that maybe it's a good time to refinance.

But how does that borrower know for sure just when it's the right time to refinance? How does the borrower know when refinancing will save money and when it will cost money? That's what we'll investigate in this chapter.

Considerations

If you're considering refinancing your property, there are a number of factors you need to consider. They include the following:

1. What is the interest rate on your current mortgage?
2. What is the current market interest rate?
3. Do you have an ARM or a fixed-rate mortgage?
4. How long do you plan to keep the property?
5. What will be your costs to refinance?
6. What is your financial condition?
7. What is your equity in the property?

Interest Rate

Usually we are only going to consider refinancing if we can get an interest rate lower than our present rate. Thus the question becomes: How much lower must the rate be before refinancing becomes practical?

A rule of thumb is that the new rate must be 3 percent or more lower than the existing rate before refinancing becomes practical.

Of course, this is just a generalization. What is considered when making the generalization are the costs involved in refinancing and the recoverability of those costs. If you plan to hold the property for a long time, then a reduction in interest rate of only 2 percent may warrant a refinance. In general, however, I would caution against a refinance if the interest rate differential were less than 2 percent and there were no other pressing needs.

Another consideration in refinancing is the revised federal income tax code, which will only allow you to deduct mortgage interest on the *original* purchase price and improvement costs. You may not be able to deduct interest charged over these amounts. You should consult an accountant for details.

ARM or Fixed Rate

In my opinion (and others will differ on this), all else being equal, a fixed-rate loan is better than an ARM. Thus, if I have an ARM, particularly one with onerous terms, I will consider refinancing. Recently, for example, I refinanced a property I own without achieving any drop in interest rate. However, I went from an ARM to a fixed-rate mortgage and considered the costs well spent.

How Long Will You Keep
the Property?

This is an important consideration. As we'll see, refinancing is costly. If we're planning to sell the property within the next year or two, the refinancing really doesn't make much sense. It's probably better to hang onto the existing loan and then simply sell. We'll save all the costs of refinancing.

Of course, if rates drop enormously (for example, more than 3 points lower than our current mortgage) we may want to reconsider.

How High Are the Refinancing Costs?

A general rule to follow is this: *It costs roughly as much to refinance as it does to buy or sell (without the real estate commission).*

In other words, refinancing is *expensive.* Here are some of the costs that we can expect to pay:

1. *Points.* The number of points charged for a refinance are the same as for a new mortgage. In some cases they may be even higher! Expect to pay anywhere from ½ to 6 points depending on market conditions at the time.

2. *Title insurance.* The lender will require a new title insurance policy. Typically this will be the more comprehensive and more costly ALTA (American Land Title Association) policy. This is based on the value of the mortgage. For a $100,000 mortgage, expect this to cost about $400 or more.

3. *Escrow.* There will have to be an escrow to handle the disbursements of funds. The fee here can vary greatly but is usually under $500.

4. *Attorney fees.* On the east coast an attorney may be required by the lender to prepare certain documents. Again the fee can vary greatly, from $25 to $500.

5. *Document preparation fees.* These fees are paid to the lender for preparing the loan documents. (I told you, lenders don't miss a trick!) This fee can be several hundred dollars.

6. *Recording fees.* These fees are paid to the county recorder for recording the loan documents. Usually recording fees are under $50.

7. *Loan origination fee.* This is a cute phrase that is equivalent to the term "points." However, by listing it separately the lender can make the borrower pay an additional point or more.

8. *Appraisal fee.* Your property must be appraised to get the mortgage. This fee is frequently paid up front at the time you make a loan application. It can be anywhere from $50 to $250.

9. *Credit check fee.* The lender calls up TRW or some other credit reporting agency, and you pay the fee. It is typically anywhere from $35 to $100.

10. *Termite inspection fee.* Most lenders require a termite clearance before they'll make a loan. Typically this costs under $100, providing no damage or infestation is found. If there is some found, then

you'll have to pay for any corrective work, which can cost from a few dollars to several thousand.

11. *Loan broker fee.*   If you used a loan broker, the fee may be listed separately. Typically such a fee is 1 point.

12. *Tax service fee.*   This is usually about $25. It simply means that if you don't pay your taxes, a company will notify the lender so it can start foreclosure.

13. *Impounds.*   The lender may require that you create an impound account to pay property taxes and insurance. (Your monthly payment is increased to cover these two items, and then the lender makes timely payment.) It can cost up to $1000 or more to set up the impound account, since it includes prepayments for taxes, insurance, utilities, etc.

A good rule of thumb to follow is that the total refinancing costs will be roughly 3 to 5 percent of the mortgage amount. If you borrow $100,000, expect it to cost $3000 to $5000 to refinance (a lot depends on the points charged).

Hints for Saving Money

There are a number of ways to save money on a refinance. If it's been a relatively short time since you purchased the property (or last refinanced it), go back to the old escrow company. Many escrow companies will only charge half for refinances of properties they've handled within the last year or two. The same holds true for title insurance companies. Use the old one and you may pay less.

Also, negotiate the costs with the lender *beforehand*. Remember, *everything* is negotiable. Try to get lower points, and if you can't, try to get the lender to cut back on some of the other costs. Surprisingly, sometimes lenders will work with you on this. Finally, when you get the loan, try to get one large enough to cover not only your existing financing and any money you may want to take out of the property, but the cost of the refinance as well. This is called capitalizing your costs. It just means that instead of paying them all at once, you're spreading them out over the life of the mortgage.

What Is Your Financial Condition?

In order to refinance, you have to requalify. It's just as if you were starting out looking for a brand new mortgage (which is what a refinance really is). Therefore, reread the first chapter to see how big a mortgage you can get. Be sure your credit rating is clear.

What Is Your Equity in the Property?

Finally, the property itself must qualify. Typically, refinances are for no more than 80 percent of market value. The lender will send out an appraiser (whose fee you will probably pay up front).

Some lenders will only refinance the amount of indebtedness you already have on the property plus the costs of the refinance. For example, if you already have a first for $50,000 and a second for $20,000, the maximum the FHA will allow on a refinance is $70,000 plus costs.

Other lenders don't care what you do with the money and will refinance up to their maximum amount (as noted, usually 80 percent of value).

Should You Refinance?

Think about it and consider the factors we've noted in this chapter. Refinancing is always costly. The real question becomes: Is it less costly to refinance or to keep my present mortgage?

To calculate the refinancing cost, add up all the costs, then see how much you will save *per year* with a lower interest rate. Finally, factor in how long you plan to own the property:

Refinance costs = years × savings in interest per year

If you can "pay off" the refinancing costs in 2 years and you plan to keep the property for 4 years, it's a good deal. On the other hand, if it takes 4 years to "pay off" the refinancing costs and you only plan to hold the property for 2, then you'll want to reconsider.

8

15-Year vs. 30-Year Mortgages

For nearly 40 years the standard term of a mortgage was 30 years. Recently, however, it has become popular to opt for shorter-term 15-year mortgages. Many lenders offer these shorter-term mortgages, sometimes for a slightly lower interest rate than their 30-year cousins.

Are 15-year mortgages better? What are their minuses as well as their pluses? Should you opt for the traditional 30-year mortgage? These and other questions will be examined in this chapter.

How the Term Affects the Monthly Payment

The "term" is the length of the mortgage. The length of the mortgage directly affects the monthly payment. To see how this works, consider the following chart:

Monthly Payments on $100,000 Mortgage at Varying Terms
12 Percent Interest

10 years	15 years	20 years	25 years	30 years	35 years
$1435	$1200	$1101	$1053	$1029	$1016

What should be obvious is that the *longer* the term of the loan, the *lower* the monthly payment. Most home buyers and other purchasers of real estate want the lowest possible monthly payment, and, since extending the term lowers the payment, they go for the longest possible term. But why was the standard set at 30 years? Why not 50 or 500?

An obvious reason is that the collateral for the mortgage is the building and most buildings wouldn't last 500 years and maybe not 100. (Studies have indicated that the actual life span of most buildings is close to 80 years.)

The not so obvious reason can be clearly seen when the monthly payments and term are plotted on a graph (see Fig. 8.1).

As we move from 10 to 15 to 20 years, we significantly reduce the monthly payment. However, as we approach a 30-year term, the amount of reduction in payment for each year added gets smaller. Once we reach 30 years, we are at the optimum point on the curve. Any further extensions of term reduce the monthly payment only insignificantly. For example, in the case of the $100,000 mortgage above, going from a 30-year term to a 35-year term, adding 5 more years to the life of the mortgage only reduces the monthly payment by about $13 a month. Going from a 30-year to a 40-year term would only reduce the monthly payment by about $20 a month for an extension of the payback period of 10 full years!

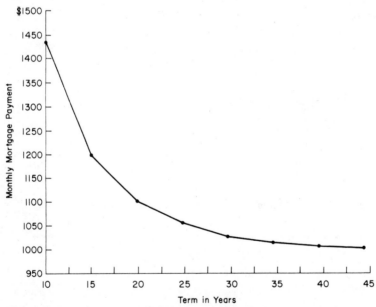

Figure 8.1. Fixed-rate mortgage: term of mortgage versus monthly payment. Monthly payments decline dramatically as term is increased until year 30. From there, further increases in term do not significantly lower payment.

It's easy to see why 30 years was chosen as the optimum payback period.

Amortization

We've seen the big picture on why a 30-year loan is the most commonly used. However, now let's look more closely at the effects of a 30-year loan on the monthly payment.

Most first mortgages on real estate are fully "amortized." That means that the payments are arranged so they are all roughly equal and the mortgage gets fully paid off. In other words, there is no balloon payment. (Occasionally the final payment may be smaller than the others.)

Table 8.1 shows what a fully amortized 30-year mortgage looks like. Note that although the monthly payment remains the same for 359 payments ($1028.62), the amount that goes toward interest and the amount that goes toward principal change with each payment. Of the first payment, only $28.62 is a return of principal, while $1000 is the interest charged. By payment 348 (year 29), however, about $900 goes to principal with only about $100 going to interest.

This means that the vast majority of the interest paid on the mortgage over its life is paid during the first years. Even after 10 years of paying, less than $100 is going to principal, more than $900 is still going to interest.

Note also that after 30 years, when the full $100,000 has been repaid, the total amount of the interest charged has been $270,016. The interest charged has been nearly three times the total amount borrowed! For higher interest rates than 12 percent, the total interest charged is also significantly higher.

How "Short" Helps

Thus far we've been considering the 30-year mortgage. However, when we switch to a 15-year mortgage, some interesting things happen. For one, when we cut the mortgage term in half, the monthly payment only goes up about 15 percent. On a $100,000 mortgage at 12 percent interest, that's an increase in monthly payment from $1029 to $1200.

Second, the total amount of interest paid is dramatically cut. Table 8.2 shows the interest on a $100,000 mortgage at 12 percent for 15 years.

Note that the total interest paid is only $116,032. That is more than half the interest that was paid over the full term on the 30-year mortgage.

In addition, each month the buyer pays more toward principal on the

Table 8.1. Amount to Principal vs. Amount
to Interest on a 30-Year Mortgage

Monthly Payment of $1028 on a $100,000
Mortgage at 12 Percent

Month	Balance	Interest	Principal
1	$99,971.30	$1000.00	$ 28.62
12	99,636.30	996.69	31.93
24	99,226.30	992.63	35.99
36	98,764.10	988.05	40.57
48	98,243.30	982.89	45.73
60	97,656.40	977.08	51.54
72	96,995.30	970.54	58.08
84	96,250.30	963.16	65.46
96	95,411.00	954.85	73.77
108	94,465.10	945.49	83.13
120	93,399.30	934.93	93.69
132	92,198.50	923.05	105.57
144	90,845.80	909.65	118.97
156	89,320.30	894.55	134.74
168	87,602.00	877.54	151.08
180	85,665.80	858.37	170.25
192	83,484.10	836.76	191.86
204	81,025.60	812.42	216.20
216	78,255.60	785.00	243.62
228	75,133.90	754.09	274.53
240	71,616.30	719.26	309.36
252	67,652.60	680.02	348.60
264	63,186.70	635.80	392.83
276	58,154.80	585.98	442.64
288	52,484.70	529.84	498.78
300	46,095.60	466.58	562.04
312	38,896.10	395.30	633.32
324	30,783.50	314.98	713.64
336	21,642.10	224.47	804.15
348	11,341.40	112.48	906.14

Final payment = $756.38
Total interest = $270,016
Total payments = $370,016

15-year mortgage. Even on the first monthly payment, nearly $200 goes
to principal as opposed to less than $30 to principal on the 30-year loan.

In other words, by opting for a short, 15-year mortgage and paying
roughly 15 percent more in monthly payments, the borrower pays the
loan off in half the time and saves more than half the interest charged
when compared with a 30-year term! Is it any wonder that many people
today are opting for the shorter 15-year mortgage?

Table 8.2. Amount to Principal vs. Amount
to Interest on a 15-Year Mortgage

Monthly Payment of $1200 on a $100,000
Mortgage at 12 Percent

Month	Balance	Interest	Principal
1	$100,000	$1002	$ 198
12	97,461	977	223
24	94,601	949	252
36	91,377	917	284
48	87,745	881	320
60	83,652	840	360
72	79,040	794	406
84	73,844	743	457
96	67,988	685	515
108	61,389	620	580
120	53,954	546	654
132	45,575	463	737
144	36,134	370	831
156	25,496	264	936
168	13,508	146	1055
180	0	12	1188

Total interest = $116,032
Total payments = $216,032

Pitfalls

Of course there are some problems here. The biggest stumbling block is
the higher monthly payment. Many borrowers simply cannot afford a
monthly payment that is 15 percent higher. What's critical to understand, in addition, is that even if you think you can afford a higher
monthly payment, you may not *always* be able to afford it.

In other words, although we may want to get a shorter-term mortgage
for the obvious advantages, chances are that over the life of that mortgage there will come a time when the payments are a real burden. Then
we may sorely wish we had the longer term and the lower payments. If
our income decreases, the short 15-year mortgage might significantly
contribute to our being forced to sell, refinance, or even lose the property.

The Better Way

There is, however, a better way of getting the benefits of a short 15-year
mortgage without losing the option of the lower payments on a 30-

year mortgage. This avenue is open to the borrower because today most mortgages do not contain prepayment penalty clauses. Rather, the mortgage frequently can be prepaid at any monthly payment. (Check your mortgage to be sure yours does, in fact, have this feature.)

With this prepayment clause we can have our cake and eat it too. Here's how it works.

We get a 30-year mortgage with a no-prepayment-penalty feature. But, we pay it off *as if it were a 15-year mortgage.* If we borrowed $100,000 at 12 percent for 30 years, our payments should be $1029 a month. However, instead of paying $1029 per month, we pay $1200 a month—$171 extra.

30-year monthly payment	$1029
Extra principal prepaid monthly	171
Total monthly payment	$1200

How It's Done

When the monthly payment stub comes from the lender, it contains two extra lines. One is for additional payments paid in advance. The second is for extra principal. On the latter we list the extra amount we are paying, thus notifying the lender that we want it to go to principal.

By paying an extra $171 per month to principal, we still in effect pay off our 30-year loan 15 years early. We will have converted our 30-year term into a 15-year term!

However, and this is the big plus, the loan is still written for 30 years with payments still set at $1029 a month. This means that at any time if the higher $1200 payments should become a burden, we can drop back down to the $1029 payments. There's no penalty for this—it's at *our* option.

The Bottom Line

Paying off a 30-year loan as if it were written for 15 years by increasing the amount to principal will work for any mortgage that has no prepayment penalty. To find the exact amount of additional principal you need to pay, check with a broker who can look up the correct monthly payment for a 15-year loan at any amount and interest rate. Or simply pay an additional 15 percent of each monthly payment for a rough figure.

If you can afford it, it really pays off in interest saved and mortgage principal reduced.

9

Qualifying for a Mortgage on Investment Property

Getting a new first mortgage on an investment property is both easier and more difficult than getting one on a residence. It's easier because the rental income from the property can help in the qualification. It's more difficult because the lenders tend to look more closely at the borrower's credit and the down payment. In this chapter we'll see how to successfully qualify for a rental house (and many other income properties).

Using Rental Income

Basically, the application procedure for a mortgage on an investment property is identical to the one for a residence. The following items, virtually identical to those for a residence, will need to be obtained and the appropriate forms filled out.

1. Loan application (Usually a Fannie Mae-Freddie Mac application is used.)

2. Credit check

3. Property appraisal

4. "Verification of deposit" from a bank or savings and loan to show that the borrower does, in fact, have the down payment in cash

5. "Verification of employment" for those who are employed or at least 2 years of tax returns for those who are self-employed

The big difference in the qualification process has to do with rental income. When we apply for a mortgage on our residence, we have to show that we can make enough to support the house. As noted in the first chapter, this is typically about 3 times or more the monthly payment for principal, interest, taxes, and insurance.

With an investment or rental property it's somewhat easier. The lender assumes that the property itself will produce income. So a percentage of that income is calculated into the figures. Here's a very rough example of how it works:

	Residence	Rental property
Monthly payment	$1000	$1000
Usual qualifying	3000	3000
Less income from property	0	1000
Needed to qualify	$3000	$2000

Since the rental income is added to our regular income, we need less income to qualify for the property.

Restrictions on Rental Income

Lenders, however, do not usually accept our estimate of what rental income will be from a given piece of property. Frequently they will make their own estimates based on the rental market. Then they typically subtract 5 percent for vacancy and another 5 percent for maintenance. Additional amounts may be subtracted if the property is deemed to need work before it can be rented.

Thus, while we may think a rental property should bring in $1000 a month, the lender may only give us $900 or less credit for it.

Don't Overlook Your Own Housing Expense

Additionally, when we qualify for an investment property we must deduct any long-term financing we have from our regular income. If we own a residence on which we are paying a mortgage, the mortgage payment (plus taxes and insurance) is deducted from our income. If we are renting, a rental allowance may be deducted. Thus, depending on how much our monthly living expenses are, it can be easier or harder to qualify for an investment property mortgage.

Finding Investment Property Mortgages

Conventional

Mortgages for investment property are available from all the lenders who regularly loan on residences. These include banks, savings and loan associations, mortgage bankers, and others.

Typically, such lenders insist on at least 20 percent down if the borrower is an investor. (The definition of an investor is someone who does not intend to live in the property but intends to rent it out.)

FHA Loans

In addition there are government loans. The most commonly used is the FHA program. FHA loans are appealing because they are fully assumable as well as being fixed-rate. A borrower who gets an FHA loan on a property usually has little trouble reselling. This is particularly appealing to investors.

In the past, FHA loans were only available to those who intended to occupy the property as their primary residence. In recent years, however, the FHA has allowed non-owner-occupied mortgages. There is, of course, a catch. While an owner-occupant typically need only put down about 5 percent, a nonresident owner must put down 15 percent of the purchase price.

The down payment for these FHA mortgages, however, no longer need be in cash. Now the seller of the property can accept a second mortgage as part of the down payment *provided that second is on other property of the borrower—not the property on which the new mortgage is going.*

There is currently a $90,000 limit on the amount of an FHA insured loan. However, there is talk of raising this ceiling in the near future. See the chapter on FHA loans for more information.

Sellers

Finally there are sellers. Sellers can be an excellent source of investor financing. They often are willing to carry back seconds or even firsts, and they usually don't even care about the borrower's credit or income. In some cases they don't even fuss that much over the down payment as long as they get their price, so it may be possible to get a 90 or even 100 percent loan here! See the chapter on creative financing for more information.

10
Graduated-Payment Mortgages

Recent studies have indicated that well over 85 percent of home purchases in this country are made by people who already own a home. What this means is that most home buyers are, in reality, "moving up." They are simply exchanging one home for another, usually of higher value.

Past home buyers are able to do this for two reasons. First, they are able to transfer their often sizable equities into the new property. This gives them a big down payment. Second, second-time homeowners frequently are individuals or families who are into their more productive years and have relatively high incomes. They can afford the high payments required of home buyers today.

But where does that leave the individuals or young couples who are the first-time home buyers? How do they, often with limited incomes and little down payment, break into the housing market?

The answer that was specifically designed for them by the lending industry is the graduated-payment mortgage (GPM). When combined with a low down payment feature, it offers reduced monthly payments in the early years of the mortgage. Then, as the borrower's income presumably grows, the monthly payments increase.

Low monthly payments when the buyer has a small income and then, gradually, higher monthly payments as the buyer's income increases. It's one method of solving the finance problem for housing.

How the GPM Works

While the GPM's basic operation is quite simple to state—low payments at first, higher payments to make up for it later on—the actual operation of the mortgage is better seen from an example.

We'll take a variety of a GPM that's been around for a few years. It is the FHA-HUD plan. This particular mortgage was intended for use as part of an FHA loan. It incorporates the low down payment feature of the FHA with the reduced-payment feature of the GPM. The mortgage is for $35,000. The down payment on the property to obtain this mortgage was only $1250. Since this first example is taken from the mid-1970s, the interest rate is only 8½ percent for 30 years (Table 10-1).*

The chart lists years from 1 through 11+. It also indicates the "level payment." The level payment is the amount that would be paid each month—if all the monthly payments were equal—in order to fully amortize the mortgage over a 30-year period. A payment of $269 per month will accomplish this.

Next to the level-payment schedule are five separate GPM payment schedules. Each has different features.

Table 10.1. Level Payment Schedule vs. GPM for a $35,000, 30-Year Loan at 8½ Percent

(U.S. Dept. of Housing and Urban Development)*

Year+	Level payment loan	GPM plans				
		1	2	3	4	5
1	$269	$245	$223	$203	$243	$223
2	269	251	234	218	248	230
3	269	257	245	234	254	237
4	269	264	258	252	258	233
5	269	270	271	271	263	251
6	269	277	284	291	269	258
7	269	277	284	291	274	266
8	269	277	284	291	280	274
9	269	277	284	291	285	282
10	269	277	284	291	291	291
11+	269	277	284	291	297	300

*From *How to Buy a Home at a Reasonable Price*, by Robert Irwin, Copyright © 1979 by McGraw-Hill. Used with permission of McGraw-Hill Book Company.

*This same mortgage is still available today, although at current interest rates.

Plan 1—Cutting the Payments

This plan offers a rate of graduation of 2½ percent for a graduation term of 5 years. This simply means that the monthly payment increases *no more* than 2½ percent per month. If we were to take 2½ percent of the first year's monthly payment of $245, we would find it is approximately $6. We then add that $6 to the $245 and we get the second year's payment of $251.

First year's payment	$245
Rate of graduation	× 0.025
Increase after 1 year	6
First year's payment	+ 245
Second year's payment	$251

The graduation period is 5 years. After that time, there is a level payment high enough to *fully amortize* the mortgage.

Under Plan 1, note that the savings are not that substantial. At year one, the year of greatest savings, only $24 a month is saved under the plan.

The savings are listed below.

Year	Savings on monthly payment
1	$24
2	18
3	12
4	5
5	−1
6+	−8

Although there's a nominal savings initially, there is also a nominal loss in terms of higher monthly payments for the last 25 years of the mortgage.

This plan might be helpful for someone who was just trying to squeeze into a home and could barely make it.

Plan 2—Cutting the Payments Lower

The term for this plan is the same term as that for Plan 1, 5 years. But Plan 2 doubles the graduation rate. It has a rate of 5 percent. Here's what the monthly savings now look like.

Year	Savings
1	$46
2	35
3	24
4	11
5	−3
6+	−15

Under Plan 2, the savings, at least in the first 2 years of the mortgage, are substantial. In year 1, the savings are 17 percent of the monthly payment.

In year 2, they are 13 percent. That's enough to make a buyer stop and consider. If you can cut your payments by 17 percent the first year and 13 percent the second, maybe it's worthwhile having that extra heavy high payment for the last 25 years of the mortgage. After all, many buyers figure that, after 5 years, they will sell the property anyhow.

Plan 3—A Radical Payment Reduction

This plan carries the whole process even further. With the same term, 5 years, it increases the graduation rate to 7½ percent. The results are dramatic:

Year	Savings
1	$66
2	51
3	24
4	17
5	−2
6+	−22

The percent savings the first year here is about 25 percent. You can cut your monthly payments by one-quarter under this plan. And they will stay lower than under a standard fixed-rate plan until year 5. After year 6, the payments will only be $22 higher than they would have been under a traditional mortgage.

It's easy to see why many people prefer this particular plan. They figure that by year 5 their income will have increased significantly and inflation will have reduced the value of the dollar to the point where they can easily afford the higher payments later.

Plans 4 and 5—Increasing the Term

Plan 4 goes back to a lower graduation rate—2 percent. But the graduation period is extended to 10 years.

What should be apparent when you look at Plan 4 is that extending the term works against the borrower more than it works for him or her. While it's true that initially the monthly payment is marginally lower, ultimately it grows significantly higher. This plan is roughly comparable to Plan 1. Yet Plan 1, which had a first-year payment within $2 a month of this plan, ended up after year 5 with a monthly payment that was $14 lower than the final monthly payment on this plan.

This discussion is not intended to confuse, but merely to illustrate once again that extending the life of the graduation, like extending the life of a mortgage, does not significantly lower the monthly payment after the first critical years.

Plan 5 again has a 10-year term, this time with a 3 percent rate of graduation.

2 percent GPM rate—10-year term	
Year	Savings
1	26
2	21
3	16
4	11
5	6
6	0
7	−5
8	−11
9	−16
10	−20
11+	−26

The FHA-HUD GPM plan has been in existence since about 1977. Other similar plans were adopted by the Federal Home Loan Bank Board for use by savings and loan associations in 1978 and 1979.

Combining the GPM with an Adjustable-Rate Mortgage

Today it is possible to combine the low initial mortgage payments of a GPM with an ARM. When this is done, the borrower typically gets very low initial payments for a set period of time. Here are the features of the GPM-ARM:

1. The mortgage typically has a graduation period between 3 and 10 years, with 5 years being the most common. What this means is that after 5 years, for example, the payments must be raised to the level where the loan is being fully amortized.

2. The maximum graduation varies between institutions, but the most common appears to be 7.5 percent. What this means is that the monthly payment is never allowed to rise by more than 7.5 percent of the previous year's monthly payment.

3. The adjustment period is commonly 1 year.

Advantages

The principal advantages of the ARM-GPM are lower initial payments *and* the fact that the borrower supposedly knows in advance exactly how much the payment is going to increase each period during the graduation time. (This is different from the straight ARM, where this is not known.)

Disadvantages

The principal disadvantage of the ARM-GPM is negative amortization. This almost invariably occurs because the payment schedule is set up so that the payment does not cover the full amount of the interest. The interest not paid accumulates and is added to the mortgage amount. Thus, as with all negative amortization, we end up owing more than we borrowed.

Limits to Negative Amortization

One of the features of the ARM-GPM not found in the fixed-rate GPM is the possibility that a lender at some future time could "recast" the loan *before* the end of the graduation period.

To understand how this could happen, we must remember that the ARM-GPM is still tied to an index. If that index should rise dramatically, then the negative amortization would also increase. Most lenders, however, will not allow the negative amortization to grow to more than 125 percent of the original loan amount. (The lender isn't being a nice guy here. It's just that 125 percent of an 80 percent loan means that the negative amortization has eaten up the buyer's entire original down payment and equity! The property, based on the original appraisal, isn't worth more than 125 percent of the original loan amount.)

If at any time the negative reaches 125 percent, the lender may "recast" the loan. This means that the loan payments will immediately be boosted up to whatever level is necessary to fully amortize (pay back) the outstanding amount.

Hidden Danger of Recasting

This presents the single greatest danger of the ARM-GPM. If interest rates skyrocket after we take out a loan and our negative amortization increases to the limit, the lender may simply recast the loan as noted above. At that point we could have monthly payment shock as our payments moved up very significantly, perhaps enough to force us into default.

ARM-GPMs offer benefits. But lurking in those benefits are also significant dangers.

Who Benefits Most from a GPM?

As noted at the beginning and indicated by the discussion of the mortgage itself, the GPM is primarily designed for buyers who anticipate having increases in their income. (While the big eye-catching feature of this mortgage is the lower initial monthly payments, it must be remembered that the monthly payments increase each year until they are substantially higher than they would have been had this been a standard loan, either fixed-rate or ARM.)

Typically, the GPM works best for a young couple or an individual in the 25 to 35 age group. This is because advancement, including increasing salary, is usually fastest in this age group.

The GPM is not recommended for those on fixed incomes or for those whose incomes are likely to remain stable or decline. Typically, this means that the GPM would be a high-risk mortgage for the individual or family in the 50-plus age group.

Advantages of the GPM

The big advantage of the GPM has already been fairly well discussed—the lower initial payments. But, perhaps it's worth remembering that this lower monthly payment has an additional bonus.

First, for the same value of house price and mortgage, the monthly payment may be reduced, thus easing the financial burden on the borrower.

Second, instead of reducing the monthly payment, the use of a GPM may mean a borrower can get a higher mortgage and a higher-priced house. For example, let's say that we've been looking at homes in the $100,000 price range. We anticipate putting $10,000 down and will thus end up with a $90,000 mortgage. At 14 percent interest, our monthly payments will be $1066 plus taxes and insurance.

We're fairly well off financially and we figure we can just make the payments. Our lender agrees that we would qualify for the mortgage. Under the conventional approach, we would look for a home at no more than $100,000 in price.

But, now let's say that we can qualify for a GPM. Under the GPM, our first year's payment will still be roughly $1066. However, this represents a 25 percent reduction from the standard mortgage payment, because of the graduated feature. For $1066 at 14 percent, we no longer are limited to a $90,000 mortgage. We can actually now afford a $120,000 mortgage and a house which costs $130,000 or more!

What I've done is not complicated, and it is well worth spending an additional moment to understand it. The emphasis thus far has been on using the GPM to *reduce* the monthly payment. What I am suggesting here is that you look at the other side of the coin and see that the reverse works equally well. The GPM can be used to keep a monthly payment (if we know what we can afford) within a budget and increase the mortgage amount and, thereby, the price we can afford to pay.

If we can only afford a $100,000 home under the traditional fixed-rate mortgage and ARM, we probably can afford a $130,000 or bigger home under the GPM. Thus the GPM broadens our horizons considerably.

Disadvantages of the GPM

High Monthly Payments Later On

The first big problem with the GPM is the fact that, in order to get lower monthly payments during the first 5 or 10 years of the mortgage, we have to accept higher monthly payments for the remainder of the mortgage. If we were to add up the savings we received during the first years of the mortgage and compare them with the amount we paid out during the remainder, we would find they were more than offset.

Savings vs. Cost of GPM

$35,000 at 8½ Percent for 30
Years at 7.5 P Graduation Rate,
5-Year Graduation Term

Year	Savings	
	Monthly	Annual
1	$66	$792
2	51	612
3	24	288
4	17	204
5	−2	−24
6–30	−22	−264

If we add up the total savings for the first 4 years, they come to $1896.

Year 1	$ 792
Year 2	612
Year 3	288
Year 4	+ 204
Total savings	$1896

Then, if we add up the total expenses, we find they come to $6360.

Year 5	$ 24
Years 6 through 30 at $264 per year	+ 6336
Total expenses	$6360

In order to save about $1900 in the first 4 years of the mortgage, we have spent over $6000 during the life of the mortgage. The net cost to us has been $4464.

Looking at it over the long term, it hardly makes sense. However, most of us don't look at the long term. The short term is the way we tend to approach these things. How many of us will actually live in the property for 30 years and pay off the mortgage? What about the effects of inflation on our money over 30 years? If we consider the short term, the loss at the end of the mortgage is more than offset by the savings at the beginning.

Problems with Negative Amortization

The second big problem with the GPM is the negative amortization. This comes up very fast. We can find that, within the first few years, our

Table 10.2. Mortgage Balance and Monthly Payment for a GPM-ARM

Year	Balance at end	Rate, %	Monthly payment	Payment increase, %	Cumulative increase, %
1	$51,362.90	13	$428.09	0	0
2	52,517.69	13	460.20	7.5	7.5
3	53,408.42	13	494.71	7.5	15.6
4	54,325.58	14.5	568.92	15	32.9
5	54,863.70	14.5	611.69	7.5	42.86
6	54,929.41	14.5	657.46	7.5	53.58
7	54,672.70	16	753.78	14.65	76.08
8	54,374.92	16	753.78	0	76.08
9	54,029.50	16	753.78	0	76.08
10	53,698.51	17.5	815.51	8.19	90.5

mortgage balance has increased 5 or even 10 percent. This can be a real problem if we have to sell, say for example, after year 3. We can find that we have far less equity in the property than we at first thought.

Of course, if we've at the same time seen a big price appreciation, we won't mind. But, if we happened to buy one of those homes in a low demand area where prices haven't really gone anywhere, by the time we pay sales closing costs and commission, we could find that after 3 years we won't even get our down payment back. In fact, it's not inconceivable that after 3 years, it might cost us money out of our pocket just to sell the property!

Consider Table 10.2 which gives figures for the ARM-GPM. Look at year 3. At that time, the mortgage value was $53,408.42. (Original value was $50,000.)

Let's say we had put 10 percent, or $5000, down into the property for a purchase price of $55,000. Now we want to sell.

The property has appreciated only 2 percent a year. It's new value is roughly $58,000.

Purchase price	$55,000
Approximate appreciation after 3 years	× 0.06
Added value	$ 3300

We have a new property value of $58,300. When it comes time to sell, we can figure that our costs including commission will be about 10 percent.

Property value after 3 years in low demand area	$58,300
Costs of sale	× .10
Sales costs including commission	$ 5830

Now, we can figure out what we are going to get back into our pocket after 3 years of ownership.

Sales price	$ 58,300
Sales costs	−5,830
	52,470
Loan balance after 3 years (negative amortization)	−53,408
Loss on sale	−938
Down payment	−5,000
Total loss during 3 years of ownership	$ −5,938

It's not a pretty picture. In this example, we would have lost nearly $6000 during our 3 years of ownership. It would have probably made more sense to rent.

Of course, the assumption we made was that we purchased in a low demand area where prices appreciated only 6 percent over 3 years. If price appreciation had been higher, say 5 to 10 percent a year, we would have come out fine. We would have gotten back our original down payment and perhaps even a profit.

The negative amortization feature of the GPM can be a disadvantage. If you get the mortgage, you want to be sure either that you're in an area of high demand and rapid appreciation *or* that you will be able to keep the house for a long time. Otherwise, be prepared to lose money when it's time to sell.

GPMs are available from a wide variety of lenders, including both banks and savings and loan associations. But, although these institutions may be authorized to offer them, not all do. For many of the more conservative lenders, GPMs are simply too difficult and too risky. Just as borrowers should be, lenders are concerned that they too may end up with a loss through foreclosure. Therefore, you may have to shop around to find them. Federally chartered savings and loans and mortgage bankers are probably your best bet.

11

Creative Financing and Second Mortgages

"Creative financing" or, as it should be called, "seller financing," has gotten bad press in recent years. Stories have been rampant about sellers who carried back financing only to lose their money and buyers who got in over their heads and lost their houses.

Many of the stories are true. Creative financing can and has been abused. It is particularly "abusable" during inflationary times. And the bad results it can create usually come to roost during recessions.

The point, however, is that creative financing has a place in the real estate market. It may even be useful to you. In this chapter we're going to scan how creative financing operates and take a look both at some of the advantages and some of the abuses.

Traditional vs. Creative Financing

Traditional financing means that a buyer goes to a lender such as a savings and loan association and borrows enough money to make a purchase. The seller receives all cash. (Of course, the seller may not get to keep all the cash. He or she probably will need to use it to pay off an existing mortgage.)

A way of defining creative financing is: financing that involves less than *all* cash to the seller or more than a single first mortgage to the buyer. In creative financing, sometimes the seller helps the buyer by giving a mortgage, but other times the seller helps only by arranging an institutional mortgage for a buyer. The best definition of creative financing, therefore, is buyer and seller working together.

The Second Mortgage for 10 Percent of the Price

Albert wanted to sell his home for $100,000, and he wanted all cash. Of course, Albert did not own his home free and clear. He actually had a mortgage on it for $18,000. But, he planned to pay off this mortgage with the proceeds from the sale and then keep the rest for himself (after closing costs and commission).

Albert listed his house for sale and waited for a buyer to come along. It took 5 months, but finally one did—Suzy.

Suzy fell in love with Albert's house. She definitely wanted to buy it. She had a good job as an officer in an insurance company and was able to qualify for a new 80 percent adjustable-rate mortgage. There was a problem, however. To buy the house, Suzy needed 20 percent, or $20,000, in cash as the down payment. She didn't have it.

The agent who represented Suzy suggested a compromise. "Why not offer the seller $90,000 cash to him and a second mortgage for the remaining $10,000?"

Suzy's cash	$ 10,000
First mortgage	+80,000
Cash to seller	90,000
Second mortgage from seller	+ 10,000
Price	$100,000

Suzy saw that she was actually borrowing from the seller the $10,000 that she needed, and in exchange giving him a $10,000 second mortgage (Figure 11.1). She agreed that the second mortgage should bear interest at 15 percent and be payable at $125 per month, and that it would be all due and payable in 3 years. (Suzy hoped that within 3 years she would be able to either sell the property or refinance with a new first mortgage for a large enough amount—$90,000—to pay off both her new first and the new second.)

Albert, at first wanted to reject the offer. After all, he wanted all cash to him. This offer would only give him 90 percent cash. The other 10 percent was paper.

Albert's agent said, "There are several advantages to this offer.

1. "You are getting your price.

2. "Even though $10,000 is in the form of a mortgage and you won't get the cash for 3 years, it will earn interest during that period. After all, if you got the $10,000 in cash, wouldn't you just stick it in the bank and earn interest on it? Here the interest is agreed upon in advance.

3. "You are selling the house."

The agent then noted the one disadvantage. "If you actually need cash, to get it you'll have to sell the mortgage to someone, and that person will normally expect a discount. The discount will probably be anywhere from 5 to 40 percent. That means if you need cash right away, you'll have to take a loss of from $500 to $4000 on the second."

Albert didn't have an immediate use for the cash and intended putting it in savings anyhow, so the second made sense for him. He agreed to the sale.

This is probably the very simplest form of creative financing that we are likely to run into. It's not particular to any time or money condition. I was writing these kinds of deals in the 1950s, just as agents are writing them today.

In the trade, they are known as 80/10/10s.

First mortgage	80%
Second mortgage	10%
Cash	+ 10%
	100%

Of course, the buyer might have gotten a 90 percent first mortgage or even a 95 percent. But, the assumption here is that, for one reason or

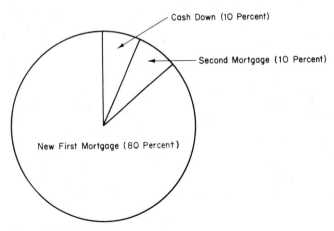

Cash Down (10 Percent)

Second Mortgage (10 Percent)

New First Mortgage (80 Percent)

Figure 11.1. Suzy's offer.

another, the buyer could qualify only for an 80 percent mortgage. Now, let's branch out into a few variations on the kind of deal we've just seen.

The Institutional Second

Let's change the situation a bit. Just prior to the signing of the sales agreement, Albert got an emergency phone call from his brother in Alaska. His brother had the opportunity of a lifetime to bid on some oil drilling contracts. But he needed cash, all the money Albert could raise.

Albert jumped at the chance and told him he would send the money right along. But, that presented a problem. Albert now needed all cash, yet the deal he was being offered was for a second mortgage for $10,000. How could he convert that $10,000 to cash without at the same time having to discount it?

Three Ways to Convert a Second Mortgage to Cash—And Avoid the Discount

"Since you now need all cash," his broker told him, "there are three ways to handle it, assuming the buyer can't come up with any more cash.

1. "Have the buyer go to a major lender such as a savings and loan association and borrow the $10,000 in a *second* mortgage. Many savings and loans are today giving short-term seconds (due in 3 to 5 years) in preference to long-term (30 years) fixed-rate firsts. They figure the short due date will help them in a volatile market. We can tell the buyer you want all cash and suggest she go out and borrow it.

"But, there is a problem. In today's market, the S&L will probably want big payments on the second. That means the buyer has to qualify for both a high-interest first *and* a high-interest second, which might be a problem. And there could still be a small discount of 4 or 5 percent.

2. "Or you could go directly to a mortgage broker (not banker) and borrow the money on a second mortgage yourself. In some cases, these mortgages are then *assumable*. You borrow the $10,000, and then the buyer *assumes* your second mortgage.

"Of course, there's the discount. In the first two ways, someone is going to have to pay a discount—usually between 4 and 12 percent. You'll get your money out this way, but you might still have to take a little bit less.

3. "There's a final way to handle this. We could jack up the price of your home a little bit, say $2000. That way, instead of getting a $10,000 second, your second mortgage would be for $12,000. Now, when you go to discount it by 20 percent, you'll be getting all your cash out ($10,000) even after the discount."

Financing the Discount

"But," Albert looked troubled, "is that fair?"

"Yes," the broker said, "if both you and the seller agree and the person you sold your second to (as well as the lender of the first) are aware of the circumstances. What we're doing here is moving the discount onto the back of the buyer. But, to make it an easy burden, it's in the form of additional amounts on the second mortgage. It's all paper, not due for another 3 years."

"I still don't get it," Albert said. "Why does increasing the price move the burden to the buyer?"

"Quite simply," the broker explained further, "we can break it down into three distinct actions:

1. "The buyer is paying more for the property, in this case $2000 more.

2. "That $2000 is not coming from the buyer in cash, nor from an additional amount of the first mortgage, but is coming in the form of an increase in the second (from $10,000 to $12,000).

3. "That increase in the second corresponds to the discount that you'll have to pay to cash out the second, so you get your money in cash."

Albert nodded.

"By paying $2000 more for the house, the buyer is paying the cost of the discount. The buyer probably won't object, however, because that $2000 is not in the form of cash from the buyer, but in the form of a second mortgage."

Finally Albert understood.

The second mortgage is a basic device used in arranging creative financing, and we'll have more to say about it in a later chapter.

But, for now, let's consider a different set of circumstances.

Using Secondary Financing to Reduce the Down and to Lower Monthly Payments

Shirley had a house she wanted to sell, and the price she was asking was $100,000. But, Shirley's house backed right up to a fire station.

Whenever there was a fire, the trucks roared out, sirens wailing. In addition to all the problems she had in selling her home in a tight market, she also had to contend with the poor location of her property.

Shirley, of course, wanted to sell for all cash. But, it quickly became apparent that no cash buyer was going to make an offer unless she lowered her price significantly, which she refused to do. So, to get her price, she was going to have to make her property somehow more appealing. How?

By offering creative financing.

Shirley has an existing first mortgage on her property for $40,000. It is an FHA loan and fully assumable.

Advantage of an Assumable First

Shirley's agent, Carl, pointed out that there was a big advantage to having an assumable first. "Your first mortgage is for 10 percent interest. That's a big incentive to a buyer in today's market where interest rates are higher."

"But," Shirley lamented, "my first is only for $40,000. I want $100,000 for my property. Where is the buyer going to get the other $60,000?"

"You're going to have to help the buyer out. You're going to have to give the buyer financing. But, it won't be so bad. You're going to get a good rate of interest on whatever mortgage you take back."

Shirley listed her house, agreeing to help with the financing. It was on the market for over 3 months without a single nibble. Carl pointed out that being near the fire station was a real drawback.

Finally, another agent brought in a potential buyer, Dorothy. Dorothy really didn't mind the fire station, and she liked Shirley's house. She wanted to buy.

However, Dorothy had some real problems.

1. She had been divorced and had two small children she was raising. Her alimony, child support, and money from a job she held only allowed her to make payments of a maximum of $800 a month, not including taxes and insurance (which she could pay extra).

2. She only had $5000 cash to put down. However, her rich uncle had died, and she expected an inheritance which she would receive within 6 months.

"Only $5000 down and with payments not more than $800 a month," Shirley wailed. "She can't possibly afford to buy my property." Shirley was convinced there could be no deal.

But Carl indicated that there might indeed be a way. "It all depends on how 'motivated' you are to sell," he said. "If you really want to get out and are willing to accept a higher risk, then we may very well be able to sell to Dorothy using creative financing."

Shirley said she did indeed want to sell and was listening closely.

Carl said that Dorothy, the buyer, had two problems—she was low on cash for an initial period of 6 months, and she couldn't afford high monthly payments. Carl asked how much the payments on the existing first mortgage (which was assumable) were.

Shirley said they were $400 a month.

"That means," Carl continued, "that Dorothy can't pay more than $400 monthly more on secondary financing. But that should be enough. I think we can work out a deal."

Here's the deal that Carl proposed (Figure 11.2).

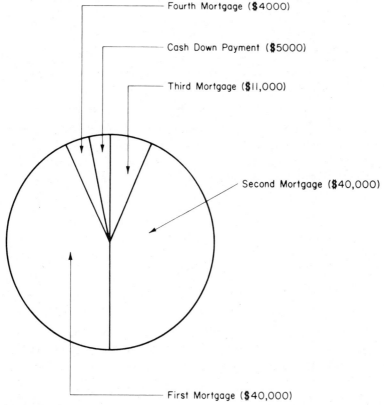

Figure 11.2. Carl's proposal.

Down payment in cash	$ 5,000
Existing first mortgage to be assumed by Dorothy	40,000
New second mortgage to be given by Shirley to Dorothy	40,000
New *third* mortgage to be given by Shirley to Dorothy	11,000
New *fourth* mortgage to be given by Shirley to Carl!	+4,000
Full purchase price	$100,000

Shirley looked at the figures and shook her head, "I don't understand this. The way you have it, I'm giving Dorothy two mortgages, a second and a third, and you're giving her a fourth. It doesn't make sense."

"It makes perfect sense," Carl said. "I'll take it one step at a time so you can see how it works."

Taking It One Step at a Time

1. "A $5000 down payment. This is easy and straightforward. Dorothy gives you $5000 down.

2. "A $40,000 first mortgage. Again, this is straightforward. This is your current first mortgage from XYZ Savings and Loan. It's FHA and assumable.

3. "A $40,000 second mortgage. Again, this is not complicated. This is the second mortgage, or the loan you are giving Dorothy to help her buy the property. We'll make it all due and payable to you in 5 years. In the meantime, you'll collect interest at 16 percent a year."

"Sixteen percent." Shirley sucked in her breath. "How much interest will that be?"

"It's easy to figure.

Second mortgage	$40,000
Interest rate	×0.16
Annual interest	6400
Months/year	÷12
Monthly interest	$ 533

"You'll be getting $6400 a year."

"I see a problem," Shirley observed. "To pay just the interest on my mortgage, it will cost $533 a month. And to pay the interest on the first mortgage, it will cost $400 a month.

Payment on first mortgage	$400
Payment on second mortgage	+533
Total payment	$933

"That means that Dorothy will need to come up with $933 a month just for the first and second. But, we already know she can't pay more than $800 a month, total. Where is she going to get the additional $133?"

"She's going to borrow it from you," Carl answered.

Shirley looked puzzled.

"It's simple. We just write the second so that the monthly payments are $400 a month, and $400 on the first and $400 on the second add up to exactly $800."

"That's just what Dorothy can afford. But, if we do that, then I won't get my full interest."

"Yes you will. We'll add the additional interest on to the second mortgage. Each month Dorothy will owe you $133 more, plus interest. It's called 'negative amortization.' (See the discussion in the previous chapter.)

Shirley nodded. "I, in effect, loan her the money to make the payments by adding it to the amount of the second mortgage."

"Precisely."

4. "Finally, there's the matter of the third mortgage."

"Yes," Shirley interrupted. "I really don't have any idea of what you're talking about there."

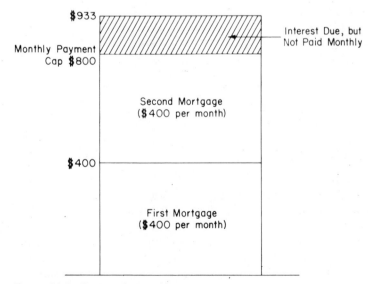

Figure 11.3. Capping the monthly payment.

When the Seller Gives the Buyer Two Mortgages on the Same House

"There can be as many mortgages as anyone is willing to lend money on property," Carl explained. "There can be first through tenth or twentieth or five hundredth. What's critical is that there be sufficient equity in the property to act as collateral for the mortgage. In the event that a borrower defaults, the first mortgage is entitled to first money, the second to second money, the third to third money, and so on. If the house is worth $100,000 and the first is $40,000, that lender in a foreclosure takes all his or her money ($40,000) out first.

"If the second is for $40,000, that lender takes all his or her money out next. If the third is for $11,000, that lender has to take what's left. If there's $9000 left, that lender gets paid some. If not, that lender and all succeeding lenders lose. (See Chapter 14 for a further discussion.)

"What I'm getting at is that there's nothing strange or unusual about having a third mortgage on a house."

"Yes," Shirley countered, "but how can I have *both* a second and a third?"

"You can have as many as you want. You could have a first, second, third, fourth, and fifth, if you and a buyer/borrower agreed."

Shirley nodded, "But what about your fourth?"

Giving the Broker a Mortgage for the Commission

"Aha," Carl smiled. "There's the matter of my commission. I'm charging you 6 percent, or $6000, to sell your home. In addition, you have closing costs to pay which will add up to about $3000. That comes to $9000. Where are you going to get the money to pay me if you are only getting $5000 in a down payment?

Closing costs and commission	$ 9000
Down payment	− 5000
Cash needed to close deal	$ − 4000

"Do you have $4000 you can let me have?"

Shirley shook her head. All her money was tied up in the property. "Besides," she replied angrily, "even if I had the money, I wouldn't want to spend it. I expect to get money out of the sale, not put it in!"

Carl nodded, "Of course. That's why we have a fourth mortgage. You'll recall that Dorothy said she expects to get a big inheritance in 6 months. I propose we make both the third and fourth mortgages due in 6 months. They will all come due and payable then. I will hold off on the payment of my $4000 commission until then, and when Dorothy pays, I'll get paid and so will you."

Shirley nodded. That kind of made sense. "Only," she added, "how can Dorothy make payments on the third and fourth mortgages? She's already up to her maximum of $800 monthly with the first and second."

Arranging It So the Buyer Has No Monthly Payments on the Mortgages

"What payments on the third and fourth?" Carl asked. There are no payments on it. It's all due and payable in 6 months, including interest at 16 percent a year.

Third mortgage amount	$11,000	$11,000
Interest rate *per year*	× 0.16	
	$ 1,760	
6 months interest		+880
Due from Dorothy in 6 months		$11,880

"At the end of 6 months, she'll pay you $11,000 plus interest. The same will happen to me and my fourth. You'll have sold your property, have cash back, plus a big second mortgage. And don't forget the extra interest you're making on the third."

Shirley nodded. It seemed better all the time. "There's just one thing. Why would Dorothy go for this deal? She's paying all kinds of interest everywhere."

"She'll go for it," Carl explained, "because it's a good deal for her. She's buying a house she likes for only $5000 down and only $800 a month (not counting taxes and insurance). Where else is she going to find a deal like that?

"Of course, there's the third she'll have to pay off plus interest. But, she's expecting the money in 6 months, so that's no big deal. And if she

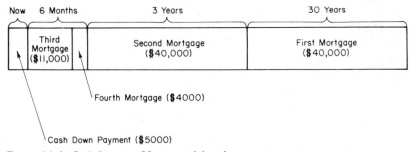

Figure 11.4. Cash flow over 30 years with low down payment.

had borrowed $15,000 to close the deal from a bank, you can be sure she would pay a lot more interest than she's paying here for such a short term.

"As far as the second mortgage is concerned, I imagine that she feels confident that within 3 years the price will go up enough so that she can refinance the house or sell to get out from under it. For Dorothy it could turn out to be as good a deal as it is for you.

The Drawback to the "Good Deal"

In the past few years, I've seen many such deals made. They are, in fact, "good deals," *if* everything works out as planned. If it doesn't, however, they can be very bad deals. My concern is that, too often, the potential disadvantages (problems that may indeed never come up) do not get pointed out. Here are some of the problems with Shirley's, Carl's, and Dorothy's deal that I see.

Possible Problems for the Buyer

From Dorothy's, the buyer's, viewpoint, the biggest single danger lies in the short-term third mortgage. True, she is expecting money in from an inheritance to pay off that mortgage. But what if there's a delay? What if the inheritance is smaller than expected? What if the inheritance taxes are larger? What if there is a legal challenge by another relative?

The "what ifs" could go on indefinitely and not one of us would live our lives if we spent all our time worrying about "what ifs." But, there's an important point to consider. It's one thing to have money in your hand, quite another to have it owed to you. Money in your hand you can spend confidently. Money owed to you can only be spent with trepidation. Dorothy ended up spending money owed to her. If it gets paid to her, she can pay Shirley and Carl. If not . . . ?

If not, Shirley and Carl would be within their rights to immediately begin foreclosure proceedings on the property and take it back from Dorothy. Dorothy would lose her new house and her down payment. (Of course, it could be argued that it won't be such a great loss since Dorothy only put up $5000.)

Possible Problems for the Seller

From Shirley's, the seller's, viewpoint, the danger lies in the small down payment that Dorothy put up. If Dorothy doesn't pay on the third, or the second, or the first, mortgages, Shirley must foreclose to protect her interest in the property. Shirley is gambling that Dorothy will pay.

She may have Dorothy's good intentions and her integrity to count on here. But, with only $5000 down, she has very little of Dorothy's money. If the inheritance doesn't work out, or if Dorothy loses her job, or her alimony or child support doesn't come in, Dorothy might just walk away.

If Dorothy walks away, that might just be the beginning of the problems for Shirley. Shirley would have to begin foreclosure proceedings. That could be costly. With lost interest payments and foreclosure costs, it could be anywhere from $2000 to $6000 or $7000. We'll say it's $5000. It could cost Shirley $5000 to foreclose and take back the house.

Of course, it might be argued that she received $5000 in down payment and so she broke even.

Wrong. Remember, there were closing costs she had to pay on the sale *including* Carl's commission!

Closing costs of sale	$ – 3,000
Carl's commission (not including fourth)	– 2,000
Foreclosure costs including	
interest payments on all mortgages	– 5,000
Total costs to Shirley	– 10,000
Down payment originally given by Dorothy	+ 5,000
Loss on attempted sale	$ – 5,000

Shirley might indeed end up with the property back, but, it also might cost her $5000 in personal expenses.

The Down Payment Is Crucial

The big point to understand here is the value of the down payment.

Institutional lenders such as savings and loan associations, banks, and others will not normally lend more than 80 percent of the purchase price of a home without some form of mortgage insurance on the amount over 80 percent.

The reason is that they intend to steer clear of the very problem that Shirley might run up against. If they do have to foreclose, that margin, that 20 percent, acts as a cushion to absorb expenses so that they don't incur any loss.

Shirley, however, because she was desperate to sell, did not maintain an adequate margin. She settled for too low a down payment to ensure her equity in the property. If Dorothy does not make her payments, Shirley loses.

How Big a Down Payment Is Minimum?

The answer to that is simple. It's an amount sufficient to cover:

1. All closing costs including commission
2. Any costs of potential foreclosure
3. Any costs of refurbishing the house and putting it on the market again
4. Any costs of effort and time on the part of Shirley in handling a possible foreclosure

That's the minimum amount. In actual dollars, it depends on the terms of each deal, but generally speaking, it is *never* less than 10 percent and is usually between 15 and 20 percent of the purchase price. Any seller accepting less is taking an additional risk.

I'm not saying that Shirley shouldn't have accepted the deal that Carl put together and that Dorothy offered. I'm merely pointing out the potential problems. You, the reader, should similarly beware of deals in which you sell property for a small down payment. Sometimes they work out beautifully. And sometimes they don't. I personally have been involved in situations that went both ways, and I can assure you that if you should have to foreclose on a deal in which you didn't get enough of a down payment, you will very quickly stop patting yourself on the back for your acumen in originally selling your property.

In a tight market, I think it's a situation in which sellers are desperate to sell take any kind of offer. But, it could be a matter of jumping out of the frying pan into the fire.

Finally, from Carl's viewpoint, this was also no terrific deal. Carl did all the work of an agent including bringing buyer and seller together. However, upon sale, Carl received only $2000 in cash. The rest he had to take in a fourth. His risk is similar to Shirley's. If Dorothy goes into default and doesn't pay on the fourth, he's not going to get his money unless he tries to foreclose. This might involve first paying off Shirley! It's a lot of effort for Carl on a not very sure thing.

An extreme form of the above transaction that has occurred in many areas of the country that involves no money down or even money back to the *buyer* upon purchase. These transactions are great, when they work. But, too often, they involve a problem that Shirley ran into—little or no money down from the buyer and a potential for foreclosure. If there *is* a foreclosure, then the seller is usually in trouble and stands to lose money.

No Money Down

In this type of transaction, the situation could be very similar to that of Shirley and Dorothy. The difference would be that, instead of Dorothy putting $5000 down, she would put nothing down. Instead, she might give Shirley a fifth mortgage for the down payment (or perhaps a promissory note).

Fifth mortgage	$ 5,000
Fourth mortgage	4,000
Third mortgage	11,000
Second mortgage	40,000
Existing first assumed	+40,000
Purchase price	$100,000

As can be seen, the deal works out in terms of the numbers. However, from a practical viewpoint, the monthly payments and payback might be

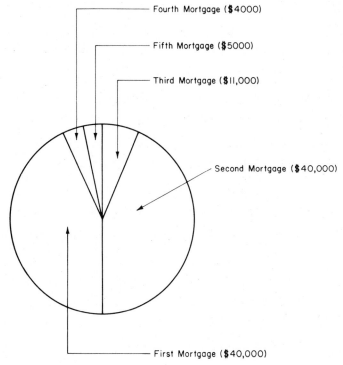

Figure 11.5. No-money-down financing.

a problem. In such deals, I've seen the payback schedule look something like this:

Fifth, due in 1 year, no interest	$ 5,000
Fourth, due in 1 year, no interest	4,000
Third, due in 2 years, 16% interest, no monthly payments	11,000
Second, due in 5 years, 16% interest, payable monthly at less than enough to pay interest, so negative amortization occurs	40,000
First assumed by buyer	+40,000
	$100,000

The seller in this situation has *no cash* from the buyer. Usually, the broker is willing to take a commission sometime in the future. To make the sale, the seller may have to actually take money out of his or her pocket to pay for closing costs.

The danger, of course, for the seller, is that, if the buyer doesn't make the payments, a foreclosure would mean more money spent (plus the cost of the commission).

In this no-money-down deal, there is increased danger, because there are no payments due on the fifth or the fourth and less than the actual amount of interest is paid on the second. This means that the buyer/borrower could actually be in trouble and have no chance of paying back the third or the fourth. But, because there are no monthly payments due, the seller might not know about it until these higher mortgages come due, a year later. Since foreclosure can take anywhere from several months to years, there could be additional costs in lost interest.

From the buyer's viewpoint, this is a house built of cards. The buyer in such circumstances usually assumes that the value of the property will go up sufficiently so that by the end of a year, he or she can refinance and get enough money to pay off the fourth and fifth.

If this doesn't happen, the buyer usually just walks away from the

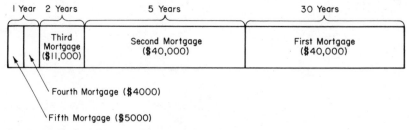

Figure 11.6. Cash flow over 30 years with no down payment.

deal. After all, the only thing the buyer has invested is the monthly payments, and if the house was rented out for the monthly payment, the buyer doesn't even have his or her own money in it at all.

Perhaps the wildest form of the no-money-down deal is the one in which the buyer actually gets cash back upon purchase. I've seen this done in at least two ways.

Money Back to Buyer on Purchase

New Homes

In one instance, builders of new homes have actually offered cash bonuses back to buyer upon the purchase of one of their homes. The homes may be selling for $200,000. The buyer puts 10 percent, or $20,000, down. The seller-contractor arranges for a lender to come up with 90 percent, or $180,000, in a first mortgage. The buyer has only one mortgage, for $180,000.

However, after the deal closes, as a bonus for buying, the contractor refunds or rebates to the buyer $25,000 to be used as the buyer wishes!

Consider this deal. The buyer puts up $20,000 and buys a home with a single first mortgage at competitive rates. Then the buyer gets $25,000 back. Even after closing costs, this buyer has really made out.

The key, of course, is the monthly payments. The buyer is stuck with a mortgage at perhaps 12 percent interest. A 12 percent interest mortgage amortized for 30 years means monthly payments of about $2000. That's a terrific burden. It means that to qualify, a buyer should be making roughly three times the monthly payment, or $6000 a month or $72,000 per year! There just aren't too many buyers in that category. What too often happens is that buyers far less able to make the monthly payments cheat on their loan application statements, buy the property, and then use the $25,000 rebate to help make their payments. They sometimes figure that if they take that $25,000 and use $1000 of it each month to offset their $2000 payment, it comes down to $1000. They can go on that way for more than 2 years before they run out of supplemental money, and then they can sell for a profit, they hope.

Maybe they can and maybe they can't. A lot depends on the market conditions at the time they decide to bail out. If they happen to end up in a very tight market, they could lose everything.

The second instance I have seen is far more complicated and, in my estimation, far more incredible.

Resale Cash Back to Buyer

Let's go back to Shirley and say that the deal she was going to make with Dorothy didn't work out. The very next day, her broker brought her a different deal. It looked like this:

New first mortgage	$ 80,000
New second mortgage to Shirley	40,000
Cash to Shirley	+20,000
Purchase price	$140,000

Shirley at first couldn't understand what was happening. The buyer was offering her $40,000 *more* than she was asking.

Carl explained it to her. "The buyer is going to get a *new* first mortgage for $80,000. Then he's going to give *you* a $40,000 second as before and $20,000 cash."

Shirley couldn't understand why the price was $140,000 when she received the same amount of money as before, $100,000.

"It's really simple," Carl said. "This buyer is going to share the proceeds of the new $80,000 first mortgage with you."

New first	$80,000
First to be paid off	−40,000
Cash	40,000
To Shirley	−20,000
To new buyer	$20,000

"Do you mean to tell me that the new buyer is actually going to get money back out of this deal?"

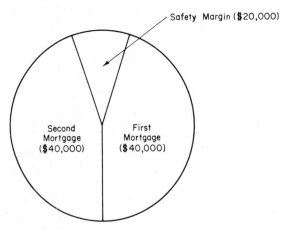

Figure 11.7. Traditional creative financing.

"That's correct," Carl said. "The buyer will put nothing into the property, but upon closing the deal, will get $20,000 in cash out."

Of course, the danger in this transaction is all to Shirley. It comes in the form of her $40,000 second mortgage. You'll recall that before, her second mortgage had as collateral her equity in the property. The house was worth $100,000, there was a $40,000 first, and the second could claim the next $40,000 of equity. She had a margin of $20,000 between her mortgage and the house's value.

Old Deal

First mortgage	$ 40,000
Second mortgage	+40,000
Total mortgages	80,000
Margin	+20,000
House value	$100,000

New Deal

First mortgage	$ 80,000
Second mortgage	+40,000
Total mortgages	120,000
House value	100,000
Margin	$ −20,000

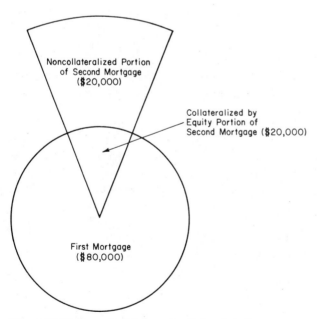

Figure 11.8. Money back to buyer/equity loss for seller.

In this new deal, Shirley would have a negative margin. That is to say, her second mortgage for $40,000 would be for $20,000 *more* than the house was actually worth! (Remember, the house didn't change value in the second deal. Regardless of the price, it still is only worth $100,000.)

The Danger to the Seller in Cash Back to Buyer

Shirley's danger here would be both real and immediate. If the buyer didn't keep up the payments and Shirley had to foreclose, not only would she be out the closing costs and possibly the commission on the sale, but she'd also stand an excellent chance of losing the $20,000 in cash the buyer got.

Her potential loss if the buyer didn't keep up the payments could amount to as much as:

Original closing costs	$ −3,000
Commission	−6,000
Costs of foreclosure including lost interest	−5,000
Loss on second mortgage because house couldn't be sold for enough to pay it off	−20,000
Total loss to Shirley	$−34,000

To sell this, *if* things don't go right for Shirley, could cost her $35,000, or more than half of her equity in the property. The downside risk here in almost every similar case I've seen far outweighs any advantage that may come from a quick sale.

From the buyer's viewpoint, I don't see how we could get a better deal. No money down, cash back on purchase, and a fairly long term (3 to 5 years) on the second.

Most buyers that I've seen using this technique have no intention of living in the property themselves. They usually intend to just rent it out and then use the monthly rental, supplemented in part by the cash back on purchase, to make their payments on the first and second mortgages. They hope that in time they'll be able to sell for enough of a profit to pay off both mortgages and leave some money left over for them.

Of course, if things don't work out, they usually feel they can walk away—and the sooner the better. After all, this buyer gets his or her profit before resale! He or she gets it the day of purchase!

Crankables

There's another variety of this technique which investors have been using of late. It involves finding a piece of property, usually a house or other residential building (two or four units), which is "crankable." The way this works is described below.

Cranking Out Cash through a Refinance

Susan is a real estate investor. She's looking for a particular piece of property. She finds it in the form of a house owned by Emerson.

Emerson has been transferred out of the state. He must sell and sell immediately. Yet, in his area, the market is very weak, and, try as he might, he can't find any buyers. After going with several agents, Emerson has lowered his price and is now trying to sell "by owner." His price is $100,000.

Susan finds Emerson's house and makes him this deal:

Existing first bought "subject to"	$ 50,000
Second "subordinated"	+ 50,000
Purchase price	$100,000

Susan is offering Emerson the full price for his property. But, she's added two new terms to the mortgages which we haven't dealt with yet. Let's consider them:

Subject to. This simply means that Susan will not assume the obligation to pay back the first mortgage. The obligation will lie with Emerson and with the house as collateral.

Subordinated. This is a very important term. When installed in a second or other junior mortgage, it means that mortgage will always remain junior or subordinate to a higher mortgage.

This really isn't very complicated. Let's say we have both a first and a second mortgage on the property. What makes the first a first and the second a second? The answer is: the time at which they were recorded. The first mortgage was first because it was recorded first in time. The second was second because it was recorded after the first.

Now, let's say that the borrower fully pays off the first mortgage. It's removed from the property. Where there had been two mortgages, there now is only one. Is that one a first or a second?

Normally, the second advances and now becomes a first. *Unless* it has been subordinated. In that case, the second would remain a second for the life of the mortgage. It would remain a second *even if there were no first before it!*

Why would Susan insist on the first being "subject to" and the second being "subordinated"?

Just in case the lender on the first mortgage had a due-on-sale clause that was enforceable, Susan might be planning not to mention anything about the sale to the lender! With a due-on-sale clause that was enforceable, if Susan attempted to assume the mortgage after a sale, it would immediately come due and payable. With a subject-to purchase, the lender might never know that the original borrower had sold the property to a new house buyer (until the transfer was recorded).

Finally, and most important, if Susan decided to "walk away" from the property, she wouldn't be liable for payment. She never *borrowed* the money. A foreclosure would not show up against her name on the first.

With regard to the second, Susan might want a subordination clause because this would make the property "crankable."

Consider, with a subordinated second, once the purchase has been made, Susan has the option of going out and getting a new first mortgage—*without paying off the existing second!*

On this property, the second, is for $50,000 and the first is for $50,000. After the purchase is consummated, Susan immediately goes out and refinances. She obtains a new first mortgage for 80 percent of the property value, or $80,000 without touching the second.

Mortgages at time of purchase

First	$ 50,000
Second	+ 50,000
Purchase price	$100,000

Mortgages after 1 month (refinanced)

First	$ 80,000
Second	+ 50,000
Total mortgage value	$130,000

By keeping the existing second mortgage in place and putting in a new, higher first mortgage, Susan has generated $30,000 in cash for herself.

New first	$80,000
Existing first paid off	− 50,000
Cash to Susan	$30,000

In the terminology of the trade, Susan has "cranked" $30,000 out of the property.

But where has that $30,000 come from? Has it come out of thin air? Remember, we said the property was worth $100,000. But now it has mortgages on it for $130,000. Did the property suddenly increase in value by $30,000?

Hardly. The cash Susan generated was directly offset by a loss in the equity protecting Emerson's second.

When property sold

Value	$100,000
Existing first	− 50,000
Equity protecting Emerson's $50,000 second	$ 50,000

When property refinanced

Value	$100,000
New first	− 80,000
Equity protecting Emerson's $50,000 second	$ 20,000

Susan has turned Emerson's collateral into cash for herself. She has cranked the property. She put nothing down and received $30,000 in cash on the refinance.

Other Crankables

Investors are always looking for crankables. They don't always have to take the form shown here. On some occasions, the investor (Susan) might leave the first and give the seller a third mortgage on the property. During times when interest rates have been very high, many sellers have been willing to lend money on thirds to get a sale without seriously considering whether there was sufficient collateral to warrant the mortgage. In such a case, the deal might look like this:

Existing first	$ 50,000
New second from outside investor	30,000
New third from seller	+ 50,000
Total mortgages on property	130,000
Property value	− 100,000
Mortgages over property value	$ 30,000

Our outside investor (usually a mortgage broker) here put up $30,000. Our seller put up $50,000 for essentially very little collateral.

Crankables worked out fine for virtually everyone when real estate prices were shooting upward in the mid to late 1970s. But, once prices stabilized during the high interest rate period that followed, the crankables didn't work. Consider it from Susan's viewpoint.

Problems with Crankables

Why should Susan continue making payments on a first and a second and even a third when she has no cash invested in the property and when the property is mortgaged for $30,000 more than its value?

There might be a moral reason, but there certainly can be no economic one, once it becomes apparent that the property isn't going to appreciate in value. So, in a tight money market, Susan and thousands of investors like her simply walk away from the property. She is saying in effect, "I'm not going to pay anymore. Sue me if you can catch me."

Now, consider the plight of Emerson, with his big third of $50,000 with only $20,000 collateral behind it. What is he to do?

He can foreclose. In Emerson's case, he would take the property back and find most of his $50,000 was gone. He only had $20,000 in equity. He would find that the foreclosure costs might be more than the equity in the property! It could cost him more to foreclose than he could recoup. He'd be better off just forgetting the whole thing.

Except for one last hope for both Emerson and the outside investor— the "deficiency judgment."

Deficiency Judgment

If either Emerson or the new investor decide to foreclose through court action (something which is not required in more than half the states), then the court will sell the property at auction to satisfy the mortgages against it.

If the property does not bring sufficient money to pay off all the mortgages, the borrower could be held personally liable for the deficiency. The court could order a "deficiency judgment," and once this was ordered, Emerson or the innocent investor could attempt to attach bank accounts and other property of Susan to recoup the money lost.

Deficiency judgments are seldom seen during times of rapid price appreciation. During periods of stability or price decline, however, they are more common. We are seeing many more deficiency judgments today than at any time during the past 40 years.

Of course, the deficiency judgment is not a panacea. To execute it, Emerson must find Susan, must find assets, and must tie them up. Along with the foreclosure process (which could take up to 2 or 3 years) the whole procedure could be very lengthy—and costly. And for Emerson there could be another roadblock, a "purchase-money law."

(A little-used section of the bankruptcy law could allow the borrower to prevent foreclosure for years and, if and when it came, prevent a deficiency judgment. Have your attorney check the bankruptcy laws if you're in that situation.)

Purchase-Money Mortgages

A good many states have purchase-money laws. Put most simply, these laws state that if a mortgage is given as part of the purchase price on a house (and sometimes other property), no deficiency judgment is allowed in the event the property sells for less than the mortgage value at a foreclosure sale.

Emerson gave Susan the $50,000 second as part of the sales price at the time of the sale. Therefore, in a state which had a purchase-money law, he probably could never secure a deficiency judgment.

Our innocent investor, however, because his was a "hard-money loan," or one that was cash advanced and not equity, might very well secure a deficiency judgment. His might not be a purchase-money mortgage.

Cranking is but one more subtype of the no-money-down, cash-back-to-buyer technique used by many buyers and investors in real estate. When crankables work out and everyone prospers, no one can knock them. But, in hard times, there's the piper to pay, and, too often, these techniques backfire on all concerned. But usually the seller is hardest hit.

Once we have the concept of crankables and no money down (or money back on purchase), the variations on the theme are almost endless and are limited only by the imagination of the investor.

Paper Down

One variation which I have seen used with increasing frequency is the "paper down." It has an interesting genesis.

Alger wanted to sell his property and Darlene wanted to buy. But, Darlene had her own house to sell before she could buy Alger's. The trouble was that Darlene had no buyers. So she came up with an interesting idea. Instead of giving Alger cash down for his property, she would give him a second mortgage on her old house. Alger's property was worth $100,000; Darlene's was worth $80,000.

Alger's sale

Second mortgage on Darlene's old house	$ 40,000
Existing first mortgage assumed by Darlene	+60,000
Purchase price	$100,000

Alger got his price and Darlene got her new house.
Of course, there's the matter of her old home.

Darlene's old home

Second in favor of Alger	$40,000
Existing first	+40,000
Value of property	$80,000

Darlene had mortgaged her old house to the hilt, and, in order to make the payments on the first and the second, she's taken it off the market and is renting it out. Because Darlene is a determined and honest person, she intends making all her payments and, eventually, when the market gets better, selling her old home and paying off Alger.

Many deals have been made in this fashion with no ill consequences. However, some enterprising investors took a look at the structure of the deal and saw that it could be adapted to something a bit less desirable.

We'll say that, at the last minute, Darlene pulled out of the deal and Alger was left still trying to sell his house. At this point, Dorene, an investor, came across it.

Dorene had just purchased a home on the following terms:

Second	$40,000
First	+40,000
Value and total mortgages	$80,000

She had bought for nothing down and she had the home mortgaged up to the full value. Now she was ready to do something with the property. She might have tried to trade it to Alger, except that he wanted to sell, not get another piece of property.

So Dorene offered Alger a $40,000 third on her property.

Dorene's offer	
First	$ 40,000
Second	40,000
Third	+40,000
Mortgages	120,000
Property value	−80,000
Mortgages in excess of property value	$ 40,000

Dorene was essentially offering Alger nothing. But he was desperate to sell, and he really didn't know property values. He only saw that she was giving him a legitimate third mortgage for $40,000 (legitimate in that the papers were all correctly drawn). He agreed to sell.

Of course, the results should be obvious. Dorene got Alger's house and $40,000 in equity in it for nothing. Alger got a worthless piece of paper on which Dorene stopped making payments. It's an old story, and it's just told here as a word to the wise about what to avoid.

Our discussion of creative financing has so far primarily involved secondary financing—second mortgages, third mortgages, and so forth.

There are other techniques, however, which are used and which do not involve this secondary financing at all. One that is gaining a lot of attention is the "rich uncle" technique.

Rich Uncle Technique

The genesis of this idea has to do with the practice of wealthy family members helping poorer family members buy homes. The poor family member bought the house; the "rich uncle" put up the down payment. Ultimately (when the house was sold) the rich uncle got his money back plus interest. The poor family member got back any appreciation.

In the modern version, there are usually two unrelated people. One is the home buyer (sometimes an investor, sometimes a person who actually intends to live in the property). The other is the "uncle," always an investor who has a lot of money to invest.

The home buyer usually qualifies for whatever financing happens to be available. The uncle puts up the down payment. They agree to keep the house for a specified period of time—usually 5 years.

At the end of that time they agree to sell the property. Out of the proceeds the uncle will first get all of his money back. Any remainder (after closing costs have been paid, of course) is usually split between home buyer and uncle.

This method, sometimes also called "sharing ownership," is helpful to the home buyer because it allows him or her to get into a property with no down payment. It is helpful to the uncle (or "aunt") because it allows him or her to get into the property with no management headaches and a percentage of the profit. Many agents promote this technique as a way to buy high-priced property when interest rates are high.

It has its drawbacks, however.

What if the property should happen not to appreciate?

Some areas of the country are experiencing depreciation or a loss of value. In this case the uncle might not only fail to receive a profit, he or she might actually end up losing all or part of the money invested!

For the home buyer, it could be just as bad. This person would end up making house payments often far higher than the rent on a comparable house, and at the end of the term, might end up with nothing to show for it!

Potentially a far more serious problem (since there is likely to be some appreciation over 5 years) is any disagreement between uncle and home buyer. The arrangement spelling out the terms between these two parties is in the form of a contract. This contract is not part of the deed to the property nor is it part of any mortgage on it. It is separate. (The co-owners do, however, usually take title to the property as "tenants in common.")

What this means is that should there be any disagreement between the two parties (over, for example, the ultimate selling price or arising out of the home buyer's sudden inability to make the monthly mortgage payments), the only solution might be litigation. The parties might have to hire attornies and fight it out in court—a costly and often lengthy experience.

Some rich uncle arrangements anticipate this problem and call for mandatory arbitration. Both parties agree to waive their rights to a lawsuit and to abide by the decision of a prenamed arbitrator. This is not always a good idea, and you should definitely consult with your attorney before signing such an agreement.

The "rich uncle" arrangement is a way to buy property using creative financing. But, like the other forms of creative financing, it has its problems.

Renting to Own

Finally, some buyers today have come up with what is a fascinating way to buy property. They rent.

What they do is to rent a piece of property on a long-term lease. Then they take out an option to buy the property at some future date. With the rental agreement, they obtain a fixed monthly payment often far lower than they would have to pay if they mortgaged the property on a normal purchase. With the option they lock in a price. Presumably when the property appreciates several years down the road, they'll exercise the option and buy at yesterday's price.

For the buyer the advantages here are great. But, there are also problems. One problem is that there is no clear title given. The lease and the option are basically contracts. While they affect the title, they do not clearly convey it. If the seller at some point down the road refuses to honor either of them, litigation is often the only answer for the buyer.

For the seller, the only advantage is getting rid of the property—and the disadvantages are enormous. Instead of selling, the seller ends up tying up the property for years. In addition, the seller agrees to sell at today's price, years into the future—simply a ridiculous commitment. And what's possibly most hazardous, in order to get some cash out of the deal for the seller, a new hard-money second is often put on the property, with the buyer agreeing to make a monthly payment sufficient to cover all mortgage, taxes, and insurance. But, if a few months down the road the buyer can't make the payments, the seller is left still holding the house. Only now it has a new big mortgage on it.

Creative Financing as a Solution

We've covered a number of methods of creative financing. But, in reality, we've only scratched the surface. There are hundreds of variations on the techniques discussed and many other techniques yet to be considered. What's important to understand is that creative financing is a mixed blessing. It can, of course, have drawbacks and be abused. But it can also mean a good sale where a sale is not possible any other way. Creative financing is not a devil by any means. But, then again, it's not an angel either.

12
Conventional Mortgages

A "conventional mortgage" is simply any loan that is not government-insured or -guaranteed. The mortgage that we get from a savings and loan association or a bank that is not an FHA or VA loan is "conventional."

The money that we get when we obtain a conventional mortgage comes directly from the lender, the bank or S&L. For example, we borrow $100,000 and the lender takes that amount of money out of its account to give to us.

However, if the lender used its own funds to finance every mortgage it made, it would soon be out of funds. Therefore, the lender, after it's made the loan, will often "sell" our mortgage to a secondary lender.

Secondary Lenders

Secondary lenders are institutions that buy up mortgages (both conventional and government) from primary lenders. These include the Federal National Mortgage Association (FNMA, often called Fannie Mae), the Federal Home Loan Mortgage Corporation (FHLMC, called Freddie Mac and also known as the Mortgage Corporation), and the Government National Mortgage Association (GNMA, or Ginnie Mae).

Between them, these three institutions undoubtedly hold the majority of home real estate mortgages in the country. The way they function is to "buy" our mortgage from our lender. Typically they will pay the lender 95 percent of the mortgage amount. The lender then has only 5 percent invested.

The lender receives interest on its 5 percent, plus it collects the payment each month and receives a fee for that. (This is the reason that most of us never know if our mortgage was resold in the secondary market.)

How the Lender Makes Its Money

Lenders who cater to the secondary market make their money in two ways. First, there's the interest received on the small amount the lender still had loaned out (typically 5 percent) and the fee for servicing the mortgage.

The other way the primary lender makes money is on points and on the interest rate "spread." The points the primary lender collects normally stay with it. That's part of its operating expenses and profit. Additionally, sometimes it is possible to sell the loan to the secondary lender at a rate slightly less than the interest rate the primary lender has coming. The primary lender, therefore, has the advantage of the spread.

Maximum Loans

The secondary lenders set specific and strict terms with regard to the loans they will make. In the first chapter we discussed qualifying. The qualifying requirements detailed there were those approved by Freddie Mac and Fannie Mae. The reason they are so commonly used is that any primary lender who wants to resell a mortgage on the secondary market must adhere to them.

These requirements are periodically changed. For example, in early 1986, Fannie Mae changed its underwriting standards in several important ways. One change was to require that the definition of "long-term debt" be changed from 6 months to 10 months. Another was to say it was sometimes willing to buy loans where the borrower qualified at a 36 percent income to monthly payment ratio.

These changes occur periodically, and it's important to check with your lender prior to obtaining financing to see what they currently are.

Additionally, the governmental agencies require the primary lenders to carry a mixture of loans—some 10 percent down, some 20 percent down, and some with even greater down payments. And finally, they set the maximum loan they will accept. Until 1985 the maximum was $116,400. However, in that year the maximum was raised to $132,400.

In 1986, it increased to $153,100. Be sure to check what the maximum secondary market loan is when you apply.

Jumbo Loans

When we apply for a mortgage, if the amount we want is at or below the maximum for the secondary lender (so the primary lender can resell it), we are usually given the best interest rate quote and the lowest points quote.

However, if the mortgage we want is higher than the maximum for the secondary market, the lender may not be able to resell it. In that case the primary lender may have to carry the loan itself.

Many large lenders are willing to do this. However, they usually charge a slightly higher interest rate and a few more points. These are frequently called "jumbo" loans.

Minimum Down Payments

In order for a lender to resell a mortgage on the secondary market, particularly if it has less than 20 percent down, the lender may be required to have that mortgage insured. The insurance is called private mortgage insurance (PMI). With PMI, until recently (and perhaps once again as you read this), it was possible to move in with as little as 5 percent down!

Private Mortgage Insurance

Private mortgage insurance companies have been around virtually since before the turn of the century, although they actually became fully legal in 1911. They were widespread during the 1920s, but their collapse during the depression led both the public and the financial community away from them. It wasn't until the mid-1950s, when a new company, the Mortgage Guarantee Insurance Corporation (MGIC), came into existence, that the field was revitalized. Today there are a dozen PMI companies across the country handling billions of dollars of business each year.

What Is PMI?

Private mortgage insurance is extraordinarily simple. It is exactly what it says it is. First of all, it's an insurance plan. It insures the person or company which lends money on a mortgage against loss. What makes PMI so unusual is that the insurer is not the government, as is the case with FHA mortgages, but rather is a private insurance company. And there you have it—private mortgage insurance.

How Does PMI Work?

The operation of PMI is easy to understand. It works almost exactly the same way as FHA insurance works. The private insurance company insures the lenders against loss for the top 20 to 25 percent of the mortgage (the lender's option).

If, for example, we have a mortgage for $60,000 which has 25 percent PMI on it, what is the amount of the insurance? The amount is 25 percent of $60,000, or $15,000. What's critical to the lender, however, is that it's the *top* $15,000. In the event the borrower got into trouble and there was a foreclosure and a loss on the property, the first $15,000 of the loss would be insured *to the lender*. Let's say that, at a foreclosure sale, the property only brought $45,000. How much money would the lender who held a $60,000 mortgage lose?

With a PMI on the property, the lender would lose nothing. The insurance company would make good the first $15,000. In this case that was the total shortage. The lender would get $45,000 from the sale and $15,000 from the insurer equaling the $60,000 mortgage liability.

On the other hand, if the property only brought $40,000, the lender would lose $5000.

Money loaned		$60,000
From sale of property	$40,000	
Maximum insurance	+ 15,000	
Lender's return	$55,000	− 55,000
Lender's loss		$ 5,000

The Insurance Premium

Of course, the private mortgage insurance company doesn't insure mortgages for nothing. It charges a fee. That fee varies from ¼ to ½ of an interest percentage point (normally it is ¼). That amount is added to the mortgage interest rate and is paid by the borrower. (If the mortgage interest rate were 10 percent, with PMI insurance at ¼ percent, the borrower would pay at 10¼ percent.) It works in exactly the same way as FHA insurance works.

Why would a borrower want to bother with PMI? After all, if you're going to have to pay 10 percent interest already, why would you want to increase that amount by another ¼ percent? It's like the straw that could break your back.

The answer has to do with lowering the down payment. PMI insurance allows the lender to lower the down payment to as little as 5 percent, and to get that low down, most borrowers are willing to pay the cost in the form of ¼ of a percent in added interest.

Qualifying for PMI

In order to get a mortgage from a lender, a borrower has to meet that lender's qualifications. In earlier chapters we suggested what those qualifications typically are.

In order for a borrower to get a 95 percent mortgage, he or she must meet not only the lender's qualifications, but the insurer's qualifications as well. The process is not lengthy or complicated, but it is rigorous.

Normally the PMI company accepts all the information directly from the lender. It looks at the standard forms that the borrower has filled out giving credit history, income, assets, property appraisal, and so forth.

The difference is that, whereas a lender might be willing to offer a mortgage at a 30 to 35 percent debt ratio (the ratio of debt to income—see page 7), a PMI company might only be willing to accept a 25 to 29 percent ratio. Where a lender might be willing to excuse a couple of late payments on a borrower's credit history, the PMI company might not. The difference is that the PMI company has to watch out for its own shirt. It's sticking its neck out and insuring the most vulnerable part of the mortgage—the first 20 or 25 percent. It wants to be very sure that the borrower is not only a good, but a great, credit risk. The same holds true with regard to the condition and location of the property.

In order to get PMI, you have to be an outstanding borrower buying an outstanding house. In order to qualify for this 5 percent down feature, you must have strong income and strong credit.

Getting Rid of the Insurance Premium

There's one additional point which should be noted about PMI from the borrower's viewpoint. Once we obtain PMI, we end up paying ¼ percent more per month on our mortgage. As we noted earlier, if our mortgage interest rate happens to be 10 percent, with the PMI policy, it becomes 10¼ percent.

What happens after we've been paying on this mortgage for a number of years and have paid it down somewhat?

The private mortgage insurance only covers the top 20 or 25 percent of the mortgage amount. If we originally took out a mortgage for 95 percent of the value of the property, and had 20 percent PMI coverage, and we've now paid that mortgage down to 75 percent of the original value, can we get the PMI removed?

Yes, we can.

Normally, once we've paid a mortgage down to about 80 percent of the original value (the appraised market value at the time the mortgage was placed on the property), we can request our lender to remove the private mortgage insurance. Most lenders will quickly comply.

The reason we would want to do this is to save that extra ¼ percent we've been paying every month. On a $60,000 mortgage, ¼ percent per month can come to about $12 cash per month. That $12 is far better in our pockets than in the insurance company's pockets.

Appreciation Doesn't Reduce PMI Coverage

This raises an interesting question. In recent years the value of homes has skyrocketed. A person who obtained a home with a $60,000 mortgage for 95 percent of the value back in 1975 probably finds that the home today might be worth $125,000. Even though the mortgage may not have been paid down to 80 percent of the *original* appraised value, the house has gone up in price to the point where perhaps the mortgage value realistically today is only half of the market value. Can the PMI be removed on the basis that the house is worth much more than the required 20 percent margin?

In most cases, no.

Realistically there is no reason to continue on with private mortgage insurance if we have a mortgage that is 80 percent or less of the true market value. But, rules are rules, and the current appraised value doesn't seem to have any influence here. It's the original appraised value that the lender, the insurance company, and the secondary lender go by.

It's not hard finding a lender willing to make 95 percent mortgages. Banks, savings and loans, and others using mortgage bankers as intermediaries will do it. Private mortgage insurance is the answer.

The difficulty is in being a strong enough buyer to qualify. In today's market, if interest rates zoom up, it becomes tough to qualify. Throw another ¼ percent for mortgage insurance on the top, and it could become impossible.

Private mortgage insurance can help. But, if it doesn't, consider the other chapters on creative financing and government-backed mortgages.

13
FHA and VA Mortgages

During the 1950s and part of the 1960s, the most popular mortgages in real estate were those offered under the Federal Housing Authority (FHA) and the Veterans Administration (VA) programs. In those days, it seemed that when a buyer bought a home, he or she first tried to get one of these mortgages. Only after this proved impossible would the buyer settle for a "conventional," or nongovernment, mortgage.

During the 1970s, however, particularly when housing prices skyrocketed, the allure of these mortgages diminished. Private Mortgage Insurance (PMI) was available to provide low down payment conventional financing. Additionally, the bureaucratic red tape made FHA-VAs less desirable choices. By the end of the 1970s, fewer than 10 percent of all mortgages were from these government programs.

Then in the 1980s the FHAs and VAs came roaring back. Assumability became important, and these loans were all assumable. In addition the maximum loan amounts were raised, making them even more attractive. Today, they are considered among the best loans a borrower can get.

FHA Mortgages

The FHA does not usually lend money to borrowers. Under the most commonly used programs, the FHA isn't even in the mortgage lending business. Instead, it insures mortgages. The borrower gets a loan from a lender, for instance, an S&L. If it's an FHA loan, the government insures payment of the mortgage to the lender. If the borrower doesn't make the payments, the FHA steps in and pays off the lender. With an FHA loan, the lender can't lose.

There are a number of FHA programs. They have included the following:

Title II

203(b)   Financing of one- to four-family dwellings

203(b)   Special financing for veterans

207   Financing rental housing and mobile home parks

221(d) Financing low-cost one- to four-family dwellings for displaced or moderate-income families

222   Financing one-family homes for service personnel

234(f)   Financing condominium units

234(d) Financing condo projects and condo conversion projects

235   Assistance to low-income families to make home purchase by subsidizing mortgage interest payments

Title I

  (b)   Financing purchase of a mobile home unit

Many of these programs have been cut or at least severely pruned as federal budget cutting has proceeded in Washington. But the basic program, 203(b), still helps finance home mortgages.

Advantages of FHA Loans

1. *They are fully assumable.* This means that, if you get one, you'll have no problem turning it over to someone else when it's time to sell the property. This feature is an enormous advantage at resale time. (*Note:* Because speculators have taken advantage of the assumability of these loans, the FHA will require, as of December 31, 1986, that lenders obtain a good credit report from the buyer before allowing assumption of an FHA loan. Similar restrictions may apply to VA loans.

2. *There are no prepayment penalties.* An FHA mortgage may be paid off in full at any time without penalty.

3. *Not only does the buyer have to qualify for the FHA mortgage, but the property has to qualify as well.* This means something more than the house simply being appraised for enough money to warrant the

mortgage. It means that the house has to qualify structurally. Sometimes on FHA mortgages, the seller will be required to bring any substandard construction up to current building codes. Any damage, such as that done by wind, water, termites, fugus, erosion, and so forth, might also have to be corrected. When a buyer purchases a home under an FHA program, he or she has virtually a government stamp of approval on it.

Disadvantages of the FHA Loan

There are some disadvantages (not many) to the FHA mortgage. These include:

1. *Maximum loan amount is $90,000 currently.*   That'll all right for some parts of the country, but for the west coast, east coast, and areas in between where residential property prices are high, it's frequently just too low for the FHA to be a useful source of financing.
2. *The borrower must occupy the property to get the low down payment.*   If we want to pay under 5 percent down, then we must be an owner-occupant. We can still get the FHA financing as a nonoccupant investor, *but* we're required to put 15 percent down.
3. *The borrower must pay a mortgage insurance premium.*   The premium is a substantial amount.

Qualifying for FHA Mortgages

The qualification procedure for an FHA mortgage is not quite the same as the one for a conventional loan. The FHA uses a different and somewhat more complex procedure. It looks something like this:

1. Total housing expenses are calculated. They must not be more than 38 percent of net income.

Net income is defined as gross income less federal income tax, and housing expenses are principal, interest, taxes, insurance, utilities. If the borrower meets the above requirement, he or she goes on to the second step in the qualification process.

2. Housing expenses are *added* to the following: alimony paid; child support payments; long-term debt.

From this figure is *subtracted:* a portion of income tax deductions (federal and state); social security income; alimony received.

The resulting figure is termed the borrower's "fixed payments." The ratio of fixed payments to net income can be no more than 53 percent to 55 percent. (Of course, good credit history, proof of employment, and verification of deposit are also required.)

If you think this is complicated, you're right! However, an easy rule of thumb to follow is that if you qualify under a 10 percent down conventional mortgage, then chances are that you probably will also qualify for an FHA mortgage.

It's also important to note that there is a great deal of gray area in the FHA qualifications. Each application is individually reviewed, and it is possible to present special evidence to avoid a negative decision.

Mortgage Premium

The mortgage insurance premium (MIP) for residential property is currently 0.038 percent of the original loan amount. (On a maximum $90,000 loan, that comes to $3420.) For a house, that money must be paid *at the time the loan is made.* That means that the buyer (usually) has to come up with an extra $3420. That could be a significant deterrent to getting the loan.

Currently, however, the MIP may be added to the mortgage amount. That is, it can be financed. On a maximum $90,000 mortgage, that means that the actual loan amount will end up being $93,420.

Note: On condominiums the FHA still allows the MIP to be paid each month or capitalized over the life of the mortgage. As of this writing, there are bills in Congress which would not only raise the MIP but would also prohibit it from being added to the loan amount or paid monthly. These bills could, if passed, conceivably kill the FHA mortgage program.

Down Payment

As noted, the down payment is 5 percent or less for owner-occupied property or 15 percent for investor-purchased. In the past, this down payment had to be in cash. Recently, however, the FHA has allowed it to be handled through secondary financing.

It works like this: If we want to buy a piece of property using an FHA mortgage, we can either put 15 percent cash down *or* we can put up a second mortgage *on a different piece of property.*

Note that the second mortgage *cannot be on the property being financed.* Rather, it has to be on some other property. For example, we may own a lot or another house. We can give the seller of the property we are currently buying a second mortgage on our other house. It may be a bit complicated, but it does work.

The FHA is part of HUD (the Department of Housing and Urban Development), with offices in all major cities and main offices in Washington, D.C.

VA Mortgages

The VA program is similar to the FHA program in that it is administered by the government. However, that's where the similarities tend to end. For new VA mortgages, the borrower has to have one vital ingredient. He or she has to be a veteran and have qualifying duty as noted below.

The biggest advantage the VA loan program has over the FHA is that in many cases there is *no down payment.* The borrower doesn't have to put up anything to make the purchase (with, of course, the exception of closing costs).

Literally millions of veterans have used the VA program. Some have gone back and used it many times. (Soon we'll see how.)

How the VA Program Works

Like an FHA mortgage, the VA loan is obtained from a lender such as a bank or S&L. However, while the FHA insures the lender against loss, the VA "guarantees" a portion of the loan. It currently guarantees the top $27,500 of the amount borrowed. If the veteran defaults, the VA will pay the first $27,500 of the debt.

Since that usually represents any loss a lender is likely to sustain, it virtually removes the lender from any risk. In actual practice, when a borrower defaults, the VA, like the FHA, buys the entire mortgage back from the lender and then tries to resell the property. (These are called VA, or FHA, "repos.") Unlike the FHA, however, if the VA sustains any loss on the resale of the property, it can come after the veteran to try to recoup its loss.

Down Payment

As of this writing, these are the *maximum* VA mortgages:

Maximum loan amount with no down = $110,000

"Little down," maximum loan amount = $135,000

The "little down" program works like this. The veteran receives a no-down mortgage up to $110,000. If the property costs more, however, the veteran can then put down 25 percent of the amount over $110,000 and the loan will handle the other 75 percent up to a total loan value of $135,000.

Entitlement

The $27,500 that the VA guarantees is called the veteran's "entitlement." When the program was first started, the entitlement was only $2000. However, housing prices have gone up, and so has the entitlement.

Reusing Entitlement

The veteran's entitlement usually remains with the vet for life. This means that if the veteran sells the property *and the VA loan is paid off*, he or she may reapply for and receive back the entitlement; he or she would then be able to get another VA loan.

Using Remaining Entitlement

Because the entitlement amount has risen, there are many veterans who bought homes years ago when the entitlement was lower and who still are eligible for a portion of their entitlement. For example, if a vet bought a home in the 1950s, when the entitlement was $5000, he or she may today be able to claim the difference between the entitlement used ($5000) and the current maximum ($27,500), or $22,500.

Qualifying for a VA Loan

Unlike the FHA or even conventional lenders, the VA does not have a hard and fast formula that it uses to qualify a veteran. Rather, it has criteria. The criteria are:

1. A history of good credit

2. Sufficient income to make the payments and support the veteran's family

3. Enough money in the bank to handle at least 6 months' worth of payments

The VA has been extremely flexible in the past regarding mortgages to vets. I have seen cases where a vet who was turned down went directly to the VA and won a reversal on the strength of a promise to make payments. A large part of the VA program has been aimed at helping veterans get a home and get started.

Eligibility Requirements

The eligibility requirements for VA loans seem to be always changing. To be sure what the current requirements are, you should check with your nearest VA office. As of this writing, vets need to have one of the following:

1. *90 days' active service* during World War II, the Korean War, or the Vietnam War

2. *180 days' continuous active service* during peacetime providing the entire time was served prior to September 7, 1980

3. *24 months' active duty* (or the enlistment period) served after September 7, 1980

Spouses of veterans may also be eligible if the husband or wife was a MIA (missing in action) or died of a service-related injury.

Children of veterans and people who received dishonorable discharges from the military do not qualify.

If you qualify and want a VA loan, you must obtain a Certificate of Eligibility (CE) from a VA office.

VA Appraisals

When a veteran applies for a mortgage, the VA appraises the property and then issues a Certificate of Reasonable Value (CRV). Sales contracts which specify that the borrower is obtaining a VA loan must also specify that if the property does not appraise for the sale price (the CRV doesn't equal the sale price), the veteran may withdraw from the sale, *or*, the veteran may opt to pay more than the CRV. However, the loan amount will still be based on the CRV, not the final sale price.

Automatics

Because of the long delays which have occurred in the past in funding VA loans, the VA has designated certain lenders to handle automatic funding. What this means is that the lender qualifies the veteran, makes the loan, and closes the deal. Then the lender secures the loan guarantee from the VA. Most large S&Ls, banks, and mortgage bankers are approved for automatics.

Owner-Occupancy Requirement

The VA has long required that the veteran plan to occupy the property. If the property is larger than a home (a duplex for example), the vet must plan to occupy one unit on the property. There are no age requirements for either VA or FHA loans.

Impound Accounts

Both VA and FHA mortgages require that the borrower establish an impound account (also called a trust fund account). This simply means that the borrower must pay for the taxes and insurance on the property on a monthly basis (i.e., must pay one-twelfth of the yearly total each month). The monthly payment goes into a lender's special impound account, and the lender pays the fees at the appropriate times each year.

14
Mortgage Instruments

We have been going on about "first," "second," "third," and other mortgages as if we were talking about hamburgers and hot dogs. But just what are these mortgage instruments that we speak of so lightly? Indeed, what are any of the mortgage devices, such as "wraparounds," whose names you may have heard bandied about? The answers are what we'll discover in this chapter.

Mortgage vs. Deed of Trust

Traditionally, in the United States, when a person wanted to borrow money and give real estate as collateral, he or she didn't get a loan. The borrower got a mortgage.

This mortgage differed significantly from other types of loans in that it specifically listed the property as collateral. There were two parties to the mortgage. There was the "mortgagor" who borrowed the money and the "mortgagee" who lent it.

Mortgages were written so that the mortgagor would have a specified amount of time in which to pay back the mortgage and interest on the money. In the event that the mortgagor for any reason was unable to pay back the money, he or she (after missing a payment or two) would be notified that they were in "default." Simply put, they were not making the payments. Once a mortgagor was in default, the mortgagee (lender) could then proceed with "foreclosure."

"Foreclosure" was the process whereby the mortgagee would wrest title away from the mortgagor and then sell the property at an open sale to the highest bidder in an attempt to recoup the money originally loaned out plus interest and expenses.

It's important to see here that the borrower or the mortgagor *did not give up title* to the property when he or she applied for a mortgage. Rather, the mortgage papers simply gave the lender or the mortgagee the right to go to court and have the court take away the mortgagor's title *if* the payment were not made.

This process of borrowing on property, but not giving up the use of the property, is technically called "hypothecation," and it is critical to borrowing on real estate.

Note: This chapter is intended only to give an overview of financing, not to provide legal advice on mortgage instruments. For any legal questions concerning mortgages or what to do in your own particular situation, you should consult with a real estate attorney.

Foreclosure

There is one significant problem with foreclosure: time. If the mortgagor fails to make the payments, the major recourse of the mortgagee (besides assessing late charges *if* called for in the mortgage document), is foreclosure. But, traditionally, in order to foreclose on a mortgage, the mortgagee has to go to court. In many cases, the mortgagor was entitled to a court trial and even a jury.

While the law may have been clear and the mortgagee may have won the court test, it took time. Depending on the state, it could have taken anywhere from a few months to a few years. During this time, the mortgag*ee* would not have the use of his or her money, nor the use of the property, nor the ability to resell the property.

Of course, it was not all peaches and cream for the mortgag*or* either. That person might also be expelled from the property pending a court outcome, and might be barred from receiving any rents.

Rights of Redemption

All in all, it was a dismal situation. What made it infinitely worse for the mortgagee was something called a "right of redemption." The old theory was that, not only was a home a person's castle, it was something as sacred as the family. Therefore, even *after* a mortgagor had lost property to a mortgagee, even after the mortgagee had gained the right to sell the property to recoup the money borrowed, in many instances the mortgagor retained the right to redeem the property *if* he or she could then come up with the original money borrowed plus interest and costs. The right of redemption in some cases existed for as long as 5 years after the formal foreclosure!

You might imagine the problems this posed for the mortga*gee*. After getting the property back, the mortgagee would naturally want to resell to get back the borrowed money. But who would buy knowing that the mortgagor might at some time in the future suddenly go back to court with sufficient funds to redeem the property? This was particularly a problem when property prices were moving up quickly and the property was worth considerably more after a few years. While the mortgagor might have easily let it go to foreclosure initially, when he or she realized it was now worth 50 percent more and there was that right of redemption in force, why not try to get it back? And the poor person who had been unwise enough to purchase while a right of redemption existed might find that suddenly the property was taken back.

Deficiency Judgment

The redemption period which benefited the mortgagor was offset in part by a benefit which the mortgagee had. When the mortgage was foreclosed through court action and the property sold to pay the loan back plus expenses, there was always the possibility that the property would not yield enough money to cover all the outstanding costs. For example, the mortgage might be for $10,000 and there might be an additional $1000 in expenses. But, when sold, the property might only yield $8000. This would amount to a loss of $3000 for the mortgagee.

However, when the mortgage was foreclosed through court action, the mortgagor might be allowed a "deficiency judgment." This meant that in the event the property did not bring enough money to pay the mortgage, the mortgagee could now go after the mortgagor's other assets. It meant that the mortgagor could be held personally liable for any loss that the mortgagee suffered on the property.

Purchase-Money Mortgages

The idea behind the deficiency judgment was that the mortgagor or borrower might have tricked the mortgagee or lender into loaning more than the property was worth. This protected the lender.

But there was another side to this. On occasion, unscrupulous sellers would sell a property to a buyer at an unconscionable price, carrying back a big mortgage. The idea was that sooner or later the buyer would discover that he or she had been cheated. At that point, the buyer would stop making payments. The mortgagee would then foreclose. But, what was more important, the mortgagee would resell the property and, since it had originally been way over price, receive far below the mortgage amount. Finally, the mortgagee would get a deficiency judgment against the mortgagor and go after his or her other property.

The whole point of this scam was that the mortgagee, by means of a false sale, could ultimately get the mortgagor's other property (not to mention a down payment and other costs).

To protect buyers from unscrupulous sellers, many states enacted "purchase-money" laws. These laws stated that *if the mortgage was part of the* purchase *price, no deficiency judgment was allowed.* Many states still have this purchase-money law in effect.

The purchase-money law is a critical factor to be aware of when we become involved in financing property. For example, in the chapter on creative financing, we saw how an unscrupulous buyer might get a seller to take back a second mortgage for far more than the house's value while slipping a bigger first underneath. (This came under the heading of cash back to buyer on sale.)

In our example, the poor seller ended up with a $40,000 mortgage with only $20,000 worth of collateral in the house. What can this seller-mortgagee do in the event the buyer-mortgagor allows the property to go into default?

Obviously, he or she can foreclose. But, just as obviously, with the house worth far less than the mortgage amount, the mortgagee isn't going to get his or her money out. The answer is to attempt to get a deficiency judgment through court action.

But, if the state in which this happens has a purchase-money law, no deficiency judgment is possible. Remember, the second mortgage was given as *part of the purchase price* and therefore comes under the law. The poor mortgagee has little recourse. And the sneaky buyer could walk away from the deal no strings attached. (And you thought real estate was all straightforward!)

Purchase-money laws are largely unchanged from the early 1930s, when many of them were enacted. But, something else fairly new has entered the arena of real estate financing—something which cured the problem of "time" involved in foreclosure. It was a new mortgage instrument which essentially *eliminated* all of the following:

1. Court foreclosure

2. Redemption

3. Deficiency judgment

This new mortgage instrument, which is being used more and more throughout the United States, is the "deed of trust."

Deed of Trust

The deed of trust (or "trust deed" as it sometimes is called) came into existence out of necessity, rather than design. The way I imagine it happening is something like this: Rachel wanted to borrow money on her property, so she went to her friend Zeke, and asked for $10,000. Zeke had the money, and he was willing to lend it. But he didn't want to get involved with the whole process of mortgage. He liked Rachel, and if she didn't pay back the money, he didn't want to have to take her to court and have a public trial. What's more, if she didn't pay, he wanted to know he would get his money back, and quickly.

Zeke thought about it for some time, then finally came up with this idea, which he discussed with Rachel.

"I'll lend you the $10,000," he began. "But I don't want a mortgage on the property. Instead, I want you to issue a deed to me."

"But," Rachel protested, "I don't want to sell. I only want to borrow."

"Yes, I know. I promise that I won't execute the deed (record it, as we'll see shortly) unless you don't make your payments. And when you fully pay off the $10,000, I'll give you your deed back."

Rachel thought about that for a while, then said, "But how can I trust you not to take my property? After all, you will have a deed to you from me in your possession."

Now it was Zeke's turn to think. After some pondering, he came up with an extraordinary idea. "Instead of making the deed out to me, you'll make it out to Parson Dithers. You trust him, don't you?"

Rachel nodded.

"You'll make out the deed to Parson Dithers and include with it instructions that he is to deed the property to me *only* if I inform him and give proof that you're not paying back the money borrowed. He'll hold it in trust for both of us. Since he's an independent third party, it would work fine."

After some consideration, Rachel agreed.

And so the trust deed might have been born.

Of course, court cases and practical application have formalized the procedure. In most cases today, there is a formal instrument, a trust deed which the borrower executes. The borrower is called the "trustor." And the person who performs Parson Dithers' job becomes the "trustee." The trustee today is usually a trust or title insurance company. And today, giving a trust deed does not infringe upon the title of the property, except to the amount of the money borrowed. That means that a borrower (trustor) can give a "first" trust deed, a "second," a "third," and so on, just as in the case of mortgages. Finally, the lender under the trust deed system is called the "beneficiary."

Today, trust deeds are used in most places in the United States. In fact, in this book, wherever we've used the term mortgage (for convenience) we might just as well have substituted the term "trust deed."

The beauty of a trust deed becomes apparent in the event the trustor does not perform up to the terms of the instrument. At that time, the beneficiary informs the trustee that the trustor is in default.

The process of foreclosure is spelled out precisely in every state. For example, in California, after a notice of default is filed, the trustor (borrower) has 90 days in which to make up all back payments, late charges, and lost interest. If the trustor does this, the trust deed is taken out of default and all is as it was before.

If, however, the trustor is not able to do this, after the 90-day waiting period, the trustee begins advertising the property for sale in a legal paper. The advertising continues for 3 weeks. During this time, the trustor may redeem the property only by *paying off* the entire mortgage amount plus any interest and costs.

Finally, after the advertising period, the property is sold "on the courthouse steps" to the highest bidder.

The trustor loses all rights to the property after the sale, including any right of redemption. The beneficiary (lender), however, loses any right to a deficiency judgment.

It works out neatly and cleanly for all concerned. (In California, at the option of the beneficiary, the trustee can go through formal court foreclosure proceedings, although this is rarely done. In that case, redemption and deficiency judgments might be allowed.)

Order of Mortgages

We've spent a lot of time talking about firsts, seconds, thirds, and so forth. But exactly what are we talking about here?

It all has to do with the process of "recording." In every county and township across the country there is an official "recorder's office." While there are several different methods of recordation, essentially it is here that the public may "record" important documents.

What does "record" mean in the case of property?

It means that a notation or a copy of the document along with the legal description of the property is placed into a book that is open to anyone to inspect. Technically, recording is called giving "constructive" notice. It's considered equivalent to advertising to the public the title condition of a piece of property.

Normally, once a document has been recorded, it is assumed that everyone knows about it (whether they've seen it or not). The reason is that they have the opportunity, if they desire, to go down to the recorder's office and find the legal description of a piece of property they are concerned about and then check the title. (In some cases, other types of notice such as advertising in a legal paper or taking physical possession may also be necessary, but that's beyond the scope of our discussion here.)

In terms of trust deeds and mortgages, this recording is critical.

When Recording Pays Off

Hal wanted to borrow $50,000 on his property, which was free and clear. He went to ABC Savings and Loan, and they agreed to give him the money in exchange for a trust deed on the property. But, at this point, a certain logistics problem occurred. They would only give him the trust deed if it were a "first." That meant that it must be the first trust deed recorded on the property. (As we saw earlier, the chronological order in which the trust deeds or mortgages are placed on the property determines the order of foreclosure. The first gets paid off fully first. Then, if there's any money left, the second gets paid off fully. Then, if any money is left, the third, and so on.)

Naturally, the lender holding a first is in the best position, and ABC wanted it. But how could they be sure that Hal hadn't already given someone else a trust deed? If he had, then automatically their trust deed would be a second or lower.

The answer is recording. It's not simply giving the trust deed that counts. It's *recording* it. The trust deed that is *recorded* first becomes the first. That *recorded* second becomes the second, and so forth.

To ensure its position, ABC Savings and Loan searched the title to be sure that Hal hadn't previously recorded any other trust deeds. Satisfied that he hadn't, they agreed to give him the money one morning at 8 A.M., but not before.

When Hal wanted to know why, they explained what they proposed to do. The recorder's office opened at 8 A.M. They would be the first there. They would quickly search the title once more to be sure he hadn't placed another trust deed on the books. If he hadn't, they would quickly record theirs, and it would immediately take effect. Then, once their position was secure, they would give him the money.

Hal's reply to this was simple. "Why should I trust you? You could record the document and then never give me the money."

ABC saw his point. So they arranged for an independent third party to handle the title search, the recording, and the dispersion of funds. This third party is called an "escrow." In addition, they arranged for title insurance, which guarantees that the escrow company did its work correctly and that the position of the first mortgage was as claimed.

And there you have it. That's how mortgages and trust deeds are recorded and how recordation determines which is first, second, third, and so forth.

More Concerns

Of course, in reality, we've only skimmed the surface. There's much more to this than meets the eye, and I would suggest that anyone involved in a mortgage who is unfamiliar with the trade consult with a real estate attorney. The attorney might look for some of the following conditions, which may or may not be in the trust deed or mortgage:

Due-on-sale clause: We've already indicated that this means the mortgage is due upon sale or transfer of title of the property.

Or more: This neat little term, when placed after the monthly payment (for example, "payable at $50 a month or more") indicates that the borrower may pay back any amount of the mortgage at any time *without a penalty.* If you want the mortgage to include a prepayment penalty, you have it written in and the "or more" taken out.

Plus interest or including interest: Here are two cute little terms which can make a big difference. "Plus interest" means that monthly payment may only be a payback of principal, with interest accruing. "Including interest" means the payment may *include* the interest.

In addition, there are other items your attorney will want to watch out for, such as a "balloon payment."

Most trust deeds and mortgages which have balloon payments don't mention it. They simply say that the borrower will pay back X dollars per month, "all due and payable in 3 years" (or whatever number of years).

It might read something like this: With a loan amount of $5000, the borrower would agree to repay, "$50 per month including 12 percent per annum interest, all due and payable in 3 years."

Does the above mortgage have a balloon payment?

It certainly does! Figure it out for yourself.

Monthly payment	$ 50	
3 years worth of payments	× 36	
Maximum amount paid back	1800	$1800
Amount borrowed	5000	
Interest rate	× 0.12	
Interest per year	600	
Number of years	× 3	
Total interest	$1800	− 1800
Principal repaid during 3-year period		$ 0

A mortgage written as above has a balloon payment of $5000 after 3 years! It is essentially an interest-only mortgage. The reason is that the monthly payment is only high enough to pay off the interest. It's not high enough to pay back the principal.

To fully amortize the above mortgage, the monthly payment would have to be $166 per month.

Beware of mortgages with unreasonably low monthly payments. Almost invariably somewhere along the line they contain a big single payment—a "balloon."

Yield

As we've noted elsewhere, junior mortgages (as seconds, thirds, and so on are sometimes called) are frequently discounted. This means that, when it comes time to sell the mortgage for cash, the lender may not be able to get the face amount. Instead, something less will be obtained.

The reason for this has to do with "yield." The yield on a mortgage is the actual amount of interest it will return. The actual amount is quite often different from the amount stated on the face of the mortgage.

It all has to do with how much money is borrowed and how much is paid back *per year* in interest.

For example, if $10,000 is borrowed at 10 percent interest for 1 year, the yield would be 10 percent. That seems fairly straightforward.

Now, however, let's say that the lender wants to sell this mortgage instrument for cash. There are buyers. But, the buyers want a yield of 20 percent, given the then current market conditions. How can the lender sell a 10 percent, $10,000 mortgage so that it will yield 20 percent?

The answer is the discount. Forgetting about amortization for a moment, we'll assume that this mortgage pays back exactly $1000 in interest over the year.

Mortgage amount	$10,000
Interest rate	× 0.10
Interest returned	$ 1000

No matter what, the total amount of interest returned on this mortgage in terms of cash is not going to be more than $1000. Yet, the person willing to buy the mortgage will buy it only if the true yield (or true interest) is 20 percent. How much does the $10,000 mortgage have to be discounted to yield a 20 percent return?

Actual cash returned	$1000
Yield desired	÷ 0.20
Discount	$5000

The answer is that the mortgage has to be discounted by $5000! This only makes sense. If someone lends out $5000 at 20 percent interest, they will indeed get back $1000 in interest over 1 year.

Mortgage amount	$5000
Interest rate	×0.20
Interest returned	$1000

Buyers of mortgages, whether they be firsts, seconds, or whatever, only speak in terms of yield. The yield they desire determines the discount they demand.

One other aspect of yield which needs to be mentioned is time. In the example above, we only considered a mortgage that yielded interest for 1 year. But, in actual practice, most mortgages, even seconds, are paid off after 3 to 5 years. This is because most property is held for only a relatively short time.

For the cash buyer of such a mortgage, this means that his or her money is going to be tied up for a considerable period of time. During that time, a new round of inflation could set in, and interest rates could shoot up. Interest rates going higher than the yield received on the second could mean an ultimate loss for this cash buyer. So most buyers of seconds will add into their price a further factor in yield for time. If our cash buyer were willing to accept a 20 percent yield on a 1-year mortgage, he or she might demand 22 percent for a 3-year mortgage or even 24 for a 5-year term.

Of course, it should be understood that these yield demands are not entirely arbitrary. They are based on the competitive cost of borrowing money in the short-term market.

It also should be understood that they work the other way as well. If you have a $10,000 second mortgage on which you are being paid 20 percent interest for 1 year and, at the time, 10 percent is considered a good yield, you might very well be able to sell the mortgage for considerably more in cash!

(If this seems all vaguely familiar to you, perhaps it's because you've been involved in the bond market. It works in a similar fashion.)

Wraparounds

Another very old type of mortgage which has come back into favor recently is the "wraparound," technically called an "all-inclusive mortgage" (AIM) or an "all-inclusive trust deed" (AITD).

The wrap was once popular for certain tax advantages it offered.

These advantages are today largely gone. But the wraparound has gained new favor for two reasons:

1. It can increase the yield to the seller on the sale of a piece of property.

2. It can give the seller increased safety.

Of course, there are many dangers inherent in the wrap, and the best advice is not to get involved in one unless you first have it checked out with a competent real estate attorney.

In general, a wraparound is much like a second mortgage, with a couple of important differences. It always involves at least one mortgage, a first usually existing on the property and perhaps one or more junior mortgages. It works like this.

Sidney has an existing 10 percent mortgage for $50,000 on her property. She is willing to carry back another $50,000 in paper to help a buyer make the purchase. (She expects the buyer to put $20,000 in cash down.) Sidney, however, instead of asking for a $50,000 second, wants a $100,000 wrap.

Our buyer is Harold. He has the down payment and he wants to buy. Only he doesn't understand what Sidney means by a wrap. She explains it to him in this fashion:

"Instead of your *assuming* my original first mortgage, and my giving you a second mortgage, you'll just buy my property *subject to* (which means you're aware of the first but not assuming payment for it) and will give me a $100,000 wrap."

Harold still looked puzzled, so Sidney continued, "You'll only have *one mortgage,* for $100,000. That's it. You'll pay me on it. And it will be a great advantage to you. Current interest rates are 15 percent, but I'll give you this wrap for only 14 percent. You'll save a whole interest point."

"But," Harold objected, "what about the first mortgage?"

"It's mine," Sidney said. "I took it out and I'll keep it. From the money you pay me, I'll make the payments on it. You won't have to worry about it."

"But what if you don't make the payments on it and the first forecloses?"

Sidney thought about that. "We'll write into the wrap that if I don't continue making the payments on the first, you have the right to assume it and make the payments and subtract them from the amount you pay me." (The first was an FHA assumable loan.)

Harold thought it over. It seemed fair, and he would be getting 1 percent lower interest than the market rate. It was a good deal, he thought.

Yield

Indeed, it probably was a good deal, although he might have wanted to look out for some problems we'll consider in a moment. But for now, let's look at the deal from Sidney's viewpoint.

Sidney is giving a $100,000 mortgage at 14 percent interest. Forgetting about amortization for the moment, that means that she will receive about $14,000 interest the first year

Mortgage amount	$100,000
Interest rate	×0.14
Interest paid first year	$ 14,000

From this amount, she will now have to make a payment on the existing first mortgage. That first, however, is at 10 percent.

Existing first	$50,000
Interest rate	×0.10
Approximate first-year interest	$ 5000
Interest received from Harold	$14,000
Interest paid on first	−5,000
Additional interest received by Sidney	$ 9,000

Because she only has to pay 10 percent on the first, her interest charges there are only $5000. But, she receives back $14,000 from Harold, giving her a net interest of $9000. Now, what is her true yield?

Remember, Sidney only advanced $50,000. (The other $50,000 was the existing first mortgage.)

Net interest	$ 9,000
Existing first	÷50,000
Yield	0.18

Sidney's true yield on the $50,000 mortgage amount she advanced (her equity in the property, which she loaned to Harold) actually came to 18 percent.

What Sidney has done, in effect, is to gain the benefit of the low interest first mortgage. If Harold had been smart, he might have said to Sidney, "I won't give you a wrap. I'll give you a second mortgage at 16 percent and I'll assume the first." He would still have been better off. *He* would have gotten the benefit of the low interest first.

Use of the wrap meant that all the benefits went to Sidney, and she managed to get the equivalent of an 18 percent yield on the money she actually loaned out.

Of course, Harold wasn't weeping. For him, there was still a single mortgage at 1 percent below market interest rates. Besides, he didn't have any idea of what he had lost out on.

Safety

Sidney had one additional reason for desiring the wrap—safety.

She really didn't trust Harold. She didn't know if he would continue making payments on the first if he assumed it. If she had given a simple second mortgage and Harold had assumed the first and then not paid, she might not have known about it for several months. Typically, institutional lenders allow their borrowers 2 to 5 months to get behind before they will actually institute foreclosure.

If the first foreclosed, Sidney, in order to protect her interests under a second, would have to then foreclose and make good all the payments on the first, including up to 5 months interest and costs.

However, because *she* was making the payment directly to the first under the wrap, she would know exactly when Harold stopped making payments, if he did. She would have far greater control. She would keep the first out of foreclosure.

(It's been my experience that some investors in real estate very quickly pick up on the concept of a wrap, while others have great difficulty with it through no fault of their own. If you're in the latter group, my suggestion is that you simply stay away from wraparounds.)

There are a few dangers inherent in the wrap of which Harold or Sidney or both may not have been aware. Some first mortgages, particularly those which may have been sold to a government secondary lender, prohibit wraps. For example, if the first was through a savings and loan association which used a due-on-sale clause, that lender might institute foreclosure proceedings as soon as it found out the property was sold.

Sidney might have set up the deal, Harold accepted, and both of them gone forward, only to find *after* the deal was closed that suddenly the first mortgage demanded immediate full payment. That could be a disaster for all concerned. It's another good reason to be sure you consult with a good attorney before getting involved in a wrap.

One last consideration is the language of the wrap. In most states, there is no formalized wraparound in the same way that there is a formalized mortgage or trust deed. Rather, it is drawn up case by case.

If your broker or seller (or buyer) draws one up well, there could be no problems. But if the document is drawn up badly, all sorts of trouble could ensue. Again, a competent attorney is the answer.

I don't mean to be scaring you away from wraps. They do have enormous advantages, both to the buyer and the seller. But, you should be aware that they, like other mortgage instruments, do have some drawbacks and pitfalls.

15

Reverse-Equity Mortgages

In recent years a new kind of mortgage has come into limited usage in a few parts of the country. It is called the "reverse-equity" or sometimes the "reverse-annuity" mortgage.

This new mortgage is primarily designed for older people, specifically those who own their homes free and clear, yet do not have enough money to live on. The loan aims to allow these people to retain ownership of their property while at the same time taking out a small portion of their equity in cash each month in order to live on.

The goals of the reverse-equity mortgage are admirable. Unfortunately, in practice the results can be quite a bit less than desirable.

How It Works

Let's take an extreme example. Harold and Rachel were both retired, yet they had no social security and no source of income other than their children. When one child died and the other divorced, however, they were cut off from all income.

They had little cash in the bank. The only thing they possessed was a paid-off house worth $100,000 in which they were living.

They went to a lender to see if they could borrow against the house. The lender nodded sympathetically as they told their story, then shook her head. They had no income on which to base a loan, hence the lender couldn't help them.

The only solution seemed to be to sell the property. However, Harold and Rachel had lived there for 30 years. They felt they were too old to move. It was their last house. They wanted to live there until they died.

Finally they found a lender that thought it could help. The lender said it didn't care about them qualifying. All it looked to was the equity in the house. It was willing to give them a mortgage that looked like this:

Reverse-Equity Mortgage

1. The full mortgage amount would be $80,000, 80 percent of the house's appraised value.

2. Harold and Rachel would not receive the $80,000 immediately. Instead they would receive $500 per month.

3. Each monthly payment they received, along with interest on it, would be subtracted from the $80,000. They would continue to receive $500 per month until they had reached the $80,000 limit. At that point they would either need to refinance or to sell the property because the loan would become due and payable.

Advantages

Harold and Rachel considered the advantages of this loan. First, they would receive in cash $500 a month, enough to pay for utilities, food, and other living expenses.

Second, they would not need to pay anything to the mortgage company. Instead, the mortgage company would just keep adding the monthly payment plus interest to the mortgage amount.

Third, they wouldn't have to sell their house, but could instead continue living in it.

To them it sounded perfect. They went for the mortgage.

Disadvantages

The problem with the reverse-equity mortgage is that, bizarre though it may be to say, the borrowers can live too long. Remember, Harold and Rachel only get the money until the payments of principal and interest add up to $80,000. At that time, they must refinance or sell. The real question is: How long will that be? Table 15.1 shows the term of this loan.

Table 15.1. Reverse-Equity Loan with
Monthly Payment to Borrower of $500

(Maximum Loan Amount Is $80,000;
Interest Rate Is 10 Percent)

Month	Payment	Principal	Interest
1	$500	$500	$4
2	500	1,004	8
3	500	1,513	13
4	500	2,025	17
5	500	2,542	21
6	500	3,063	26
12	500	6,283	52
18	500	9,667	81
24	500	13,223	110
30	500	16,962	141
36	500	20,891	174
42	500	25,021	209
48	500	29,361	245
54	500	33,923	283
60	500	38,719	323
66	500	43,758	365
72	500	49,056	409
78	500	54,623	455
84	500	60,475	504
90	500	66,626	555
96	500	73,091	609
102	500	79,885	666
	$51,000	$80,000	$29,551

Years = 8.5

It takes a surprisingly short time, only 8.5 years, for the amount lent to
Harold and Rachel to add up to $80,000. The reason, of course, is that
old nemesis, interest paid on interest. With this type of loan the borrowers pay an increasing interest penalty.

Consider. Assuming the interest is 10 percent, the first month the
interest is $50 on $500 loaned. The second month, however, the borrowers pay on the next $500 loaned plus the $550 previously loaned; the
interest is $55. Each month the interest amount rises. Very quickly it
overwhelms the principal.

Opinion

In my opinion the reverse-equity mortgage can be a cruel hoax played
on those who are most vulnerable. It eats up capital (equity) at a fero-

cious rate, and if the borrowers are unfortunate(!) enough to outlive the mortgage, they are nearly penniless *and* in a position where they may have to move anyway.

Limiting the Reverse-Equity Mortgage

Lenders, realizing the possible adverse effects of a reverse-equity mortgage, have been slow to embrace it. Very few are offered. In some cases where they have been offered, there has been an attempt to link them up with an insurance policy. The insurance policy, however, does not work in the way we would expect it to. It pays off only if the borrowers outlive the mortgage, and then it only pays interest to the lender on the money loaned until the borrowers do die and the property can be sold.

Quite frankly, because of the bizarre nature of this kind of insurance, it is not easy to find. (This type of arrangement, however, is not new. It once was common in Europe. An older person would pledge property to a younger one. The terms were that the younger person would take care of the older one until the person's death. Then the property would transfer. Unfortunately, sometimes the older person lived beyond the younger person's patience, and then some very suspicious deaths occurred.)

A Better Idea

The whole idea behind the reverse-equity mortgage is to allow the older person(s) to remain in the property and at the same time receive income from their equity. At least one of these goals, however, may be better left unattained than accomplished: remaining in the property.

If the older people do move from the house, then they can do one of two things. (1) They can sell it and receive part of the sales price in cash and part in a mortgage which will give them money to live on and pay them income each month. (2) They can refinance, then move out and rent the property. The rental income could pay for the refinance, leaving them the cash to invest or to live on.

The key, however, is that the older person must be willing to move. Having dealt with parents and grandparents who did not want to move and having found ways to allow them to stay in their homes, I can say from personal experience that staying is not necessarily the best way.

Ultimately, when illness strikes, they may have to move anyway, and then to a convalescent hospital.

Sometimes a move, though very painful and disconcerting, can be a better choice than staying with a financially unstable situation.

In any event it is a difficult choice to make, and I have great sympathy for relatives as well as older individuals who are forced to make it.

16

Steps to Getting a New Mortgage

If you've read this book through to here, you undoubtedly are now a bit of an expert on mortgages. However, there is one question of a practical nature that you may still be unable to answer. "How do I actually go out and get a new mortgage?" We'll clear that up right away.

Where to Look

Here are the lenders who offer mortgages. You can call them by phone (usually the quickest way to get answers), or drop by. These people are in the business of lending money, and they will be delighted to talk with you:

1. Savings and loan associations
2. Banks
3. Mortgage bankers
4. Mortgage brokers

There are other sources, such as insurance companies, but generally they operate through mortgage bankers. Banks and S&Ls are easily understood. For those unfamiliar with them, however, mortgage bankers and brokers may need some explaining.

Mortgage Bankers

A mortgage *broker* is a person who contacts a number of lenders, then, for a fee (sometimes paid by the borrower, sometimes by the lender), arranges a mortgage. Mortgage brokers are usually real estate agents who have moved into the mortgage field.

Mortgage bankers, on the other hand, work differently. These people actually lend their own money. Then they resell the mortgage either to a secondary lender (such as Fannie Mae) or to another primary lender (such as an out-of-state S&L). Their fee almost always comes from the lender rather than from the borrower.

Mortgage bankers and brokers are listed in the phone book under Real Estate Loans. You can usually tell the bankers from the brokers because the former will plainly state that they are "bankers" in their ad. In any event, it's a good idea to ask if they lend their own money and if they charge the borrower a fee.

What to Ask

Here are some of the questions you will want to ask any lender. (Also look at Chapter 4 for specific questions to ask regarding an ARM.)

1. Will you lend up to the amount, $_____, I need?

2. What interest rate will you charge?

3. Is it a fixed-rate loan or an ARM?

4. What are the points?

5. What is the term of the loan?

6. Can you "lock in," or guarantee, the points and the interest rate? If so, when does the lock-in start? Does it start right now, when I fill out a loan application, or when the lender approves the loan? (Usually the sooner the better.)

7. What "up front fees" do you require? (Usually they are the cost of the credit report and appraisal. Be suspicious of anything else.)

8. On a refinance, will your loan cover both my existing mortgages and the cost of the refinance? Will it allow me to cash in part of my equity? How much?

9. How long will it take from the time I fill out an application until the loan can be funded?

10. How will you handle any special problems (such as inadequate income or credit difficulties) that I may have?

The Procedure

After you've located a lender you feel will do the job for you, the procedure is fairly standard. Here are the steps:

1. Fill out a loan application.

2. Give the signed application to the lender's representative with payment for a credit report and appraisal. (These fees are some times waived.)

3. Get a "verification of employment" to your employer. The employer will need to fill it out and then mail it directly back to the lender.

4. Get a "verification of deposit" from your bank showing your bank accounts and that you have enough money to handle the property.

5. If you are self-employed, get copies of at least 2 years' worth of complete federal tax returns and send to the lender.

6. Wait for the appraisal and credit report to come back.

7. Wait.

8. Wait.

9. Wait a bit longer.

10. Call the lender and ask what's holding up the show. You will be told the appraisers are busy, the lender is busy, the credit reporting company is busy . . .

11. If the credit report is okay and the appraisal is for enough, and you've supplied the verifications and/or tax returns, the lender will call one day and say the mortgage package is complete and is going to "committee." That means that your loan will be brought before the senior officers of the lender and they will either approve or deny it. If it's come this far, the chances of approval are 99 percent.

12. Open escrow (if you haven't already done so).

13. The lender calls and says the loan is approved. It will now take anywhere from 1 or 2 days to several weeks for the lender to fill out the necessary forms and send them to the escrow. Calling on the phone daily and badgering the lender to hurry up will sometimes help, sometimes produce the opposite result of that desired.

14. The escrow officer says the documents are in. Go down, sign the documents (after reading them carefully and perhaps getting an attorney's opinion). Escrow closes, and you get the money (or have

it applied toward the purchase or refinance of a piece of property).

10.1. The lender calls and says the appraisal is too low or the credit report is bad. Ask for a reappraisal (it's about all you can do) from a different appraiser. You may have to pay again for this.

10.2. The lender calls and says there is a problem (or problems) with the credit report. Fix the bad credit report. You will be given a copy. It will show what the problems are. Creditors may be saying you paid late or didn't repay at all.

   Your alternatives begin with a letter by you to the lender explaining your side of the problem. Sometimes these will suffice. Sometimes you'll have to call the creditors, pay them off, and get them to change the report, if they will. Sometimes nothing will work.

10.3. The lender turns you down because of poor credit. This doesn't necessarily mean you can't buy property. Just go out looking for an existing FHA or VA loan that you can assume.

You've Done It!

And that's all there is to it. Of course, I hope that you've studied the terms that lenders used and are able to get a low interest rate, few points, and favorable terms. All of which is to say that if you turned here first, now it's time to go back and read the rest of this book!

Appendix

Mortgage Finder

How to Use the Mortgage Finder

The tables in this appendix are probably unlike any you've seen before. They can be used to find the following information*:

1. *To find maximum price you can pay given the maximum monthly payment you can afford*—read down "Monthly Payment" to the maximum you can afford, then right to "Maximum Price."

2. *To find your total monthly payment for a specific purchase price*—read down "Maximum Price" column to your purchase price, then left to "Monthly Payment" column to see the monthly payment including principal, interest, taxes, and insurance.

3. *To find the approximate income needed to qualify for a particular mortgage*—read down "Maximum Amount" to your mortgage amount, then right to "Income To Qualify" column.

4. *To find approximate maximum price you can afford given your income*—read down "Income To Qualify" until you find your income, then read left to "Maximum Price."

Special note: These tables assume that the mortgage is fixed rate for 30 years, you are putting 20 percent down, lenders require that no more than 33 percent of income be used for net monthly payment (principal, interest, taxes and insurance) and that taxes and insurance will be 2 percent of the purchase price annually. (In addition, gross monthly payment – net payment plus long term debt – cannot exceed 36 percent of income.)

If you should put only 10 percent down (instead of 20 percent), many of the figures in these tables will not apply. (The amount of monthly payment for principal and interest for any given loan amount, however, will still remain accurate.)

Additionally on the west coast, particularly California, where property taxes tend to be low, the payment shown may be a bit high. In parts of the midwest and east coast where property taxes tend to be higher, the payment shown may be a bit low.

For these reasons, these tables must only be taken as *approximations*. The actual figures you encounter may be somewhat different.

5. *To find the maximum mortgage amount given the purchase price—* read down the column marked "Maximum Price" to your price, then over to the left to the column marked "Maximum Amount."

6. *To find the approximate maximum mortgage you can get given your income—*read down the column marked "Income To Qualify" to your income, then over to the left to "Maximum Amount."

7. *To find the maximum purchase price given a specific mortgage amount—*read down "Maximum Amount" column, then right to "Maximum Price" column.

8. *To find the principal and interest only monthly payment for a mortgage amount—*read down "Maximum Amount" column, then right to "Mortgage P & I" column.

7% Interest, 30-Year Term, 20% Down

(2% of purchase price assumed for taxes and insurance; 33% of gross monthly income allowed for mortgage payment)

Monthly payment	Maximum mortgage		Maximum price	Income to qualify	
	Amount	P & I		Monthly	Annual
$349	$40,000	$266	$50,000	$1,048	$12,581
$363	$41,600	$277	$52,000	$1,090	$13,084
$377	$43,200	$287	$54,000	$1,132	$13,587
$391	$44,800	$298	$56,000	$1,174	$14,091
$405	$46,400	$309	$58,000	$1,216	$14,594
$419	$48,000	$319	$60,000	$1,258	$15,097
$433	$49,600	$330	$62,000	$1,300	$15,600
$447	$51,200	$341	$64,000	$1,342	$16,104
$461	$52,800	$351	$66,000	$1,384	$16,607
$475	$54,400	$362	$68,000	$1,426	$17,110
$489	$56,000	$373	$70,000	$1,468	$17,613
$503	$57,600	$383	$72,000	$1,510	$18,116
$517	$59,200	$394	$74,000	$1,552	$18,620
$531	$60,800	$405	$76,000	$1,594	$19,123
$545	$62,400	$415	$78,000	$1,636	$19,626
$559	$64,000	$426	$80,000	$1,677	$20,129
$573	$65,600	$436	$82,000	$1,719	$20,633
$587	$67,200	$447	$84,000	$1,761	$21,136
$601	$68,800	$458	$86,000	$1,803	$21,639
$615	$70,400	$468	$88,000	$1,845	$22,142
$629	$72,000	$479	$90,000	$1,887	$22,646
$643	$73,600	$490	$92,000	$1,929	$23,149
$657	$75,200	$500	$94,000	$1,971	$23,652
$671	$76,800	$511	$96,000	$2,013	$24,155
$685	$78,400	$522	$98,000	$2,055	$24,659
$699	$80,000	$532	$100,000	$2,097	$25,162
$713	$81,600	$543	$102,000	$2,139	$25,665
$727	$83,200	$554	$104,000	$2,181	$26,168
$741	$84,800	$564	$106,000	$2,223	$26,671
$755	$86,400	$575	$108,000	$2,265	$27,175
$769	$88,000	$585	$110,000	$2,306	$27,678
$783	$89,600	$596	$112,000	$2,348	$28,181
$797	$91,200	$607	$114,000	$2,390	$28,684
$811	$92,800	$617	$116,000	$2,432	$29,188
$825	$94,400	$628	$118,000	$2,474	$29,691
$839	$96,000	$639	$120,000	$2,516	$30,194
$853	$97,600	$649	$122,000	$2,558	$30,697
$867	$99,200	$660	$124,000	$2,600	$31,201
$881	$100,800	$671	$126,000	$2,642	$31,704
$895	$102,400	$681	$128,000	$2,684	$32,207
$909	$104,000	$692	$130,000	$2,726	$32,710
$923	$105,600	$703	$132,000	$2,768	$33,214
$937	$107,200	$713	$134,000	$2,810	$33,717

Monthly payment	Maximum mortgage		Maximum price	Income to qualify	
	Amount	P & I		Monthly	Annual
$951	$108,800	$724	$136,000	$2,852	$34,220
$965	$110,400	$735	$138,000	$2,894	$34,723
$979	$112,000	$745	$140,000	$2,936	$35,227
$992	$113,600	$756	$142,000	$2,977	$35,730
$1,006	$115,200	$766	$144,000	$3,019	$36,233
$1,020	$116,800	$777	$146,000	$3,061	$36,736
$1,034	$118,400	$788	$148,000	$3,103	$37,239
$1,048	$120,000	$798	$150,000	$3,145	$37,743
$1,062	$121,600	$809	$152,000	$3,187	$38,246
$1,076	$123,200	$820	$154,000	$3,229	$38,749
$1,090	$124,800	$830	$156,000	$3,271	$39,252
$1,104	$126,400	$841	$158,000	$3,313	$39,756
$1,118	$128,000	$852	$160,000	$3,355	$40,259
$1,132	$129,600	$862	$162,000	$3,397	$40,762
$1,146	$131,200	$873	$164,000	$3,439	$41,265
$1,160	$132,800	$884	$166,000	$3,481	$41,769
$1,174	$134,400	$894	$168,000	$3,523	$42,272
$1,188	$136,000	$905	$170,000	$3,565	$42,775
$1,202	$137,600	$916	$172,000	$3,607	$43,278
$1,216	$139,200	$926	$174,000	$3,648	$43,782
$1,230	$140,800	$937	$176,000	$3,690	$44,285
$1,244	$142,400	$947	$178,000	$3,732	$44,788
$1,258	$144,000	$958	$180,000	$3,774	$45,291
$1,272	$145,600	$969	$182,000	$3,816	$45,794
$1,286	$147,200	$979	$184,000	$3,858	$46,298
$1,300	$148,800	$990	$186,000	$3,900	$46,801
$1,314	$150,400	$1,001	$188,000	$3,942	$47,304
$1,328	$152,000	$1,011	$190,000	$3,984	$47,807
$1,342	$153,600	$1,022	$192,000	$4,026	$48,311
$1,356	$155,200	$1,033	$194,000	$4,068	$48,814
$1,370	$156,800	$1,043	$196,000	$4,110	$49,317
$1,384	$158,400	$1,054	$198,000	$4,152	$49,820
$1,398	$160,000	$1,065	$200,000	$4,194	$50,324

7½% Interest, 30-Year Term, 20% Down

(2% of purchase price assumed for taxes and insurance; 33% of gross monthly income allowed for mortgage payment)

Monthly payment	Maximum mortgage Amount	P & I	Maximum price	Income to qualify Monthly	Annual
$363	$40,000	$280	$50,000	$1,089	$13,069
$378	$41,600	$291	$52,000	$1,133	$13,592
$392	$43,200	$302	$54,000	$1,176	$14,115
$407	$44,800	$313	$56,000	$1,220	$14,638
$421	$46,400	$324	$58,000	$1,263	$15,160
$436	$48,000	$336	$60,000	$1,307	$15,683
$450	$49,600	$347	$62,000	$1,350	$16,206
$465	$51,200	$358	$64,000	$1,394	$16,729
$479	$52,800	$369	$66,000	$1,438	$17,251
$494	$54,400	$380	$68,000	$1,481	$17,774
$508	$56,000	$392	$70,000	$1,525	$18,297
$523	$57,600	$403	$72,000	$1,568	$18,820
$537	$59,200	$414	$74,000	$1,612	$19,342
$552	$60,800	$425	$76,000	$1,655	$19,865
$566	$62,400	$436	$78,000	$1,699	$20,388
$581	$64,000	$448	$80,000	$1,743	$20,911
$595	$65,600	$459	$82,000	$1,786	$21,433
$610	$67,200	$470	$84,000	$1,830	$21,956
$624	$68,800	$481	$86,000	$1,873	$22,479
$639	$70,400	$492	$88,000	$1,917	$23,002
$653	$72,000	$503	$90,000	$1,960	$23,525
$668	$73,600	$515	$92,000	$2,004	$24,047
$683	$75,200	$526	$94,000	$2,048	$24,570
$697	$76,800	$537	$96,000	$2,091	$25,093
$712	$78,400	$548	$98,000	$2,135	$25,616
$726	$80,000	$559	$100,000	$2,178	$26,138
$741	$81,600	$571	$102,000	$2,222	$26,661
$755	$83,200	$582	$104,000	$2,265	$27,184
$770	$84,800	$593	$106,000	$2,309	$27,707
$784	$86,400	$604	$108,000	$2,352	$28,229
$799	$88,000	$615	$110,000	$2,396	$28,752
$813	$89,600	$627	$112,000	$2,440	$29,275
$828	$91,200	$638	$114,000	$2,483	$29,798
$842	$92,800	$649	$116,000	$2,527	$30,321
$857	$94,400	$660	$118,000	$2,570	$30,843
$871	$96,000	$671	$120,000	$2,614	$31,366
$886	$97,600	$682	$122,000	$2,657	$31,889
$900	$99,200	$694	$124,000	$2,701	$32,412
$915	$100,800	$705	$126,000	$2,745	$32,934
$929	$102,400	$716	$128,000	$2,788	$33,457
$944	$104,000	$727	$130,000	$2,832	$33,980
$958	$105,600	$738	$132,000	$2,875	$34,503
$973	$107,200	$750	$134,000	$2,919	$35,025

Monthly payment	Maximum mortgage		Maximum price	Income to qualify	
	Amount	P & I		Monthly	Annual
$987	$108,800	$761	$136,000	$2,962	$35,548
$1,002	$110,400	$772	$138,000	$3,006	$36,071
$1,016	$112,000	$783	$140,000	$3,049	$36,594
$1,031	$113,600	$794	$142,000	$3,093	$37,117
$1,046	$115,200	$806	$144,000	$3,137	$37,639
$1,060	$116,800	$817	$146,000	$3,180	$38,162
$1,075	$118,400	$828	$148,000	$3,224	$38,685
$1,089	$120,000	$839	$150,000	$3,267	$39,208
$1,104	$121,600	$850	$152,000	$3,311	$39,730
$1,118	$123,200	$861	$154,000	$3,354	$40,253
$1,133	$124,800	$873	$156,000	$3,398	$40,776
$1,147	$126,400	$884	$158,000	$3,442	$41,299
$1,162	$128,000	$895	$160,000	$3,485	$41,821
$1,176	$129,600	$906	$162,000	$3,529	$42,344
$1,191	$131,200	$917	$164,000	$3,572	$42,867
$1,205	$132,800	$929	$166,000	$3,616	$43,390
$1,220	$134,400	$940	$168,000	$3,659	$43,913
$1,234	$136,000	$951	$170,000	$3,703	$44,435
$1,249	$137,600	$962	$172,000	$3,747	$44,958
$1,263	$139,200	$973	$174,000	$3,790	$45,481
$1,278	$140,800	$985	$176,000	$3,834	$46,004
$1,292	$142,400	$996	$178,000	$3,877	$46,526
$1,307	$144,000	$1,007	$180,000	$3,921	$47,049
$1,321	$145,600	$1,018	$182,000	$3,964	$47,572
$1,336	$147,200	$1,029	$184,000	$4,008	$48,095
$1,350	$148,800	$1,040	$186,000	$4,051	$48,617
$1,365	$150,400	$1,052	$188,000	$4,095	$49,140
$1,380	$152,000	$1,063	$190,000	$4,139	$49,663
$1,394	$153,600	$1,074	$192,000	$4,182	$50,186
$1,409	$155,200	$1,085	$194,000	$4,226	$50,708
$1,423	$156,800	$1,096	$196,000	$4,269	$51,231
$1,438	$158,400	$1,108	$198,000	$4,313	$51,754
$1,452	$160,000	$1,119	$200,000	$4,356	$52,277

8% Interest, 30-Year Term, 20% Down

(2% of purchase price assumed for taxes and insurance; 33% of gross monthly income allowed for mortgage payment)

Monthly payment	Maximum mortgage Amount	Maximum mortgage P & I	Maximum price	Income to qualify Monthly	Income to qualify Annual
$377	$40,000	$294	$50,000	$1,131	$13,567
$392	$41,600	$305	$52,000	$1,176	$14,109
$407	$43,200	$317	$54,000	$1,221	$14,652
$422	$44,800	$329	$56,000	$1,266	$15,195
$437	$46,400	$340	$58,000	$1,311	$15,737
$452	$48,000	$352	$60,000	$1,357	$16,280
$467	$49,600	$364	$62,000	$1,402	$16,823
$482	$51,200	$376	$64,000	$1,447	$17,365
$497	$52,800	$387	$66,000	$1,492	$17,908
$513	$54,400	$399	$68,000	$1,538	$18,451
$528	$56,000	$411	$70,000	$1,583	$18,993
$543	$57,600	$423	$72,000	$1,628	$19,536
$558	$59,200	$434	$74,000	$1,673	$20,079
$573	$60,800	$446	$76,000	$1,718	$20,621
$588	$62,400	$458	$78,000	$1,764	$21,164
$603	$64,000	$470	$80,000	$1,809	$21,707
$618	$65,600	$481	$82,000	$1,854	$22,249
$633	$67,200	$493	$84,000	$1,899	$22,792
$648	$68,800	$505	$86,000	$1,945	$23,335
$663	$70,400	$517	$88,000	$1,990	$23,877
$678	$72,000	$528	$90,000	$2,035	$24,420
$693	$73,600	$540	$92,000	$2,080	$24,962
$708	$75,200	$552	$94,000	$2,125	$25,505
$724	$76,800	$564	$96,000	$2,171	$26,048
$739	$78,400	$575	$98,000	$2,216	$26,590
$754	$80,000	$587	$100,000	$2,261	$27,133
$769	$81,600	$599	$102,000	$2,306	$27,676
$784	$83,200	$611	$104,000	$2,352	$28,218
$799	$84,800	$622	$106,000	$2,397	$28,761
$814	$86,400	$634	$108,000	$2,442	$29,304
$829	$88,000	$646	$110,000	$2,487	$29,846
$844	$89,600	$657	$112,000	$2,532	$30,389
$859	$91,200	$669	$114,000	$2,578	$30,932
$874	$92,800	$681	$116,000	$2,623	$31,474
$889	$94,400	$693	$118,000	$2,668	$32,017
$904	$96,000	$704	$120,000	$2,713	$32,560
$920	$97,600	$716	$122,000	$2,759	$33,102
$935	$99,200	$728	$124,000	$2,804	$33,645
$950	$100,800	$740	$126,000	$2,849	$34,188
$965	$102,400	$751	$128,000	$2,894	$34,730
$980	$104,000	$763	$130,000	$2,939	$35,273
$995	$105,600	$775	$132,000	$2,985	$35,816
$1,010	$107,200	$787	$134,000	$3,030	$36,358

Monthly payment	Maximum mortgage		Maximum price	Income to qualify	
	Amount	P & I		Monthly	Annual
$1,025	$108,800	$798	$136,000	$3,075	$36,901
$1,040	$110,400	$810	$138,000	$3,120	$37,444
$1,055	$112,000	$822	$140,000	$3,166	$37,986
$1,070	$113,600	$834	$142,000	$3,211	$38,529
$1,085	$115,200	$845	$144,000	$3,256	$39,072
$1,100	$116,800	$857	$146,000	$3,301	$39,614
$1,115	$118,400	$869	$148,000	$3,346	$40,157
$1,131	$120,000	$881	$150,000	$3,392	$40,700
$1,146	$121,600	$892	$152,000	$3,437	$41,242
$1,161	$123,200	$904	$154,000	$3,482	$41,785
$1,176	$124,800	$916	$156,000	$3,527	$42,328
$1,191	$126,400	$928	$158,000	$3,573	$42,870
$1,206	$128,000	$939	$160,000	$3,618	$43,413
$1,221	$129,600	$951	$162,000	$3,663	$43,956
$1,236	$131,200	$963	$164,000	$3,708	$44,498
$1,251	$132,800	$974	$166,000	$3,753	$45,041
$1,266	$134,400	$986	$168,000	$3,799	$45,584
$1,281	$136,000	$998	$170,000	$3,844	$46,126
$1,296	$137,600	$1,010	$172,000	$3,889	$46,669
$1,311	$139,200	$1,021	$174,000	$3,934	$47,212
$1,327	$140,800	$1,033	$176,000	$3,980	$47,754
$1,342	$142,400	$1,045	$178,000	$4,025	$48,297
$1,357	$144,000	$1,057	$180,000	$4,070	$48,840
$1,372	$145,600	$1,068	$182,000	$4,115	$49,382
$1,387	$147,200	$1,080	$184,000	$4,160	$49,925
$1,402	$148,800	$1,092	$186,000	$4,206	$50,468
$1,417	$150,400	$1,104	$188,000	$4,251	$51,010
$1,432	$152,000	$1,115	$190,000	$4,296	$51,553
$1,447	$153,600	$1,127	$192,000	$4,341	$52,096
$1,462	$155,200	$1,139	$194,000	$4,387	$52,638
$1,477	$156,800	$1,151	$196,000	$4,432	$53,181
$1,492	$158,400	$1,162	$198,000	$4,477	$53,724
$1,507	$160,000	$1,174	$200,000	$4,522	$54,266

8½% Interest, 30-Year Term, 20% Down

(2% of purchase price assumed for taxes and insurance; 33% of gross monthly income allowed for mortgage payment)

Monthly payment	Maximum mortgage Amount	P & I	Maximum price	Income to qualify Monthly	Annual
$391	$40,000	$308	$50,000	$1,173	$14,073
$407	$41,600	$320	$52,000	$1,220	$14,636
$422	$43,200	$332	$54,000	$1,267	$15,199
$438	$44,800	$344	$56,000	$1,313	$15,761
$453	$46,400	$357	$58,000	$1,360	$16,324
$469	$48,000	$369	$60,000	$1,407	$16,887
$485	$49,600	$381	$62,000	$1,454	$17,450
$500	$51,200	$394	$64,000	$1,501	$18,013
$516	$52,800	$406	$66,000	$1,548	$18,576
$532	$54,400	$418	$68,000	$1,595	$19,139
$547	$56,000	$431	$70,000	$1,642	$19,702
$563	$57,600	$443	$72,000	$1,689	$20,265
$579	$59,200	$455	$74,000	$1,736	$20,828
$594	$60,800	$468	$76,000	$1,783	$21,391
$610	$62,400	$480	$78,000	$1,829	$21,953
$625	$64,000	$492	$80,000	$1,876	$22,516
$641	$65,600	$504	$82,000	$1,923	$23,079
$657	$67,200	$517	$84,000	$1,970	$23,642
$672	$68,800	$529	$86,000	$2,017	$24,205
$688	$70,400	$541	$88,000	$2,064	$24,768
$704	$72,000	$554	$90,000	$2,111	$25,331
$719	$73,600	$566	$92,000	$2,158	$25,894
$735	$75,200	$578	$94,000	$2,205	$26,457
$751	$76,800	$591	$96,000	$2,252	$27,020
$766	$78,400	$603	$98,000	$2,299	$27,583
$782	$80,000	$615	$100,000	$2,345	$28,145
$797	$81,600	$627	$102,000	$2,392	$28,708
$813	$83,200	$640	$104,000	$2,439	$29,271
$829	$84,800	$652	$106,000	$2,486	$29,834
$844	$86,400	$664	$108,000	$2,533	$30,397
$860	$88,000	$677	$110,000	$2,580	$30,960
$876	$89,600	$689	$112,000	$2,627	$31,523
$891	$91,200	$701	$114,000	$2,674	$32,086
$907	$92,800	$714	$116,000	$2,721	$32,649
$923	$94,400	$726	$118,000	$2,768	$33,212
$938	$96,000	$738	$120,000	$2,815	$33,775
$954	$97,600	$750	$122,000	$2,861	$34,337
$969	$99,200	$763	$124,000	$2,908	$34,900
$985	$100,800	$775	$126,000	$2,955	$35,463
$1,001	$102,400	$787	$128,000	$3,002	$36,026
$1,016	$104,000	$800	$130,000	$3,049	$36,589
$1,032	$105,600	$812	$132,000	$3,096	$37,152
$1,048	$107,200	$824	$134,000	$3,143	$37,715

Monthly payment	Maximum mortgage		Maximum price	Income to qualify	
	Amount	P & I		Monthly	Annual
$1,063	$108,800	$837	$136,000	$3,190	$38,278
$1,079	$110,400	$849	$138,000	$3,237	$38,841
$1,095	$112,000	$861	$140,000	$3,284	$39,404
$1,110	$113,600	$874	$142,000	$3,331	$39,967
$1,126	$115,200	$886	$144,000	$3,377	$40,529
$1,141	$116,800	$898	$146,000	$3,424	$41,092
$1,157	$118,400	$910	$148,000	$3,471	$41,655
$1,173	$120,000	$923	$150,000	$3,518	$42,218
$1,188	$121,600	$935	$152,000	$3,565	$42,781
$1,204	$123,200	$947	$154,000	$3,612	$43,344
$1,220	$124,800	$960	$156,000	$3,659	$43,907
$1,235	$126,400	$972	$158,000	$3,706	$44,470
$1,251	$128,000	$984	$160,000	$3,753	$45,033
$1,267	$129,600	$997	$162,000	$3,800	$45,596
$1,282	$131,200	$1,009	$164,000	$3,847	$46,159
$1,298	$132,800	$1,021	$166,000	$3,893	$46,721
$1,313	$134,400	$1,033	$168,000	$3,940	$47,284
$1,329	$136,000	$1,046	$170,000	$3,987	$47,847
$1,345	$137,600	$1,058	$172,000	$4,034	$48,410
$1,360	$139,200	$1,070	$174,000	$4,081	$48,973
$1,376	$140,800	$1,083	$176,000	$4,128	$49,536
$1,392	$142,400	$1,095	$178,000	$4,175	$50,099
$1,407	$144,000	$1,107	$180,000	$4,222	$50,662
$1,423	$145,600	$1,120	$182,000	$4,269	$51,225
$1,439	$147,200	$1,132	$184,000	$4,316	$51,788
$1,454	$148,800	$1,144	$186,000	$4,363	$52,351
$1,470	$150,400	$1,156	$188,000	$4,409	$52,913
$1,485	$152,000	$1,169	$190,000	$4,456	$53,476
$1,501	$153,600	$1,181	$192,000	$4,503	$54,039
$1,517	$155,200	$1,193	$194,000	$4,550	$54,602
$1,532	$156,800	$1,206	$196,000	$4,597	$55,165
$1,548	$158,400	$1,218	$198,000	$4,644	$55,728
$1,564	$160,000	$1,230	$200,000	$4,691	$56,291

9% Interest, 30-Year Term, 20% Down

(2% of purchase price assumed for taxes and insurance; 33% of gross monthly income allowed for mortgage payment)

Monthly payment	Maximum mortgage Amount	Maximum mortgage P & I	Maximum price	Income to qualify Monthly	Income to qualify Annual
$405	$40,000	$322	$50,000	$1,216	$14,587
$421	$41,600	$335	$52,000	$1,264	$15,170
$438	$43,200	$348	$54,000	$1,313	$15,754
$454	$44,800	$360	$56,000	$1,361	$16,337
$470	$46,400	$373	$58,000	$1,410	$16,921
$486	$48,000	$386	$60,000	$1,459	$17,504
$502	$49,600	$399	$62,000	$1,507	$18,088
$519	$51,200	$412	$64,000	$1,556	$18,671
$535	$52,800	$425	$66,000	$1,605	$19,255
$551	$54,400	$438	$68,000	$1,653	$19,838
$567	$56,000	$451	$70,000	$1,702	$20,422
$583	$57,600	$463	$72,000	$1,750	$21,005
$600	$59,200	$476	$74,000	$1,799	$21,588
$616	$60,800	$489	$76,000	$1,848	$22,172
$632	$62,400	$502	$78,000	$1,896	$22,755
$648	$64,000	$515	$80,000	$1,945	$23,339
$665	$65,600	$528	$82,000	$1,994	$23,922
$681	$67,200	$541	$84,000	$2,042	$24,506
$697	$68,800	$554	$86,000	$2,091	$25,089
$713	$70,400	$566	$88,000	$2,139	$25,673
$729	$72,000	$579	$90,000	$2,188	$26,256
$746	$73,600	$592	$92,000	$2,237	$26,840
$762	$75,200	$605	$94,000	$2,285	$27,423
$778	$76,800	$618	$96,000	$2,334	$28,007
$794	$78,400	$631	$98,000	$2,383	$28,590
$810	$80,000	$644	$100,000	$2,431	$29,174
$827	$81,600	$657	$102,000	$2,480	$29,757
$843	$83,200	$669	$104,000	$2,528	$30,341
$859	$84,800	$682	$106,000	$2,577	$30,924
$875	$86,400	$695	$108,000	$2,626	$31,508
$891	$88,000	$708	$110,000	$2,674	$32,091
$908	$89,600	$721	$112,000	$2,723	$32,674
$924	$91,200	$734	$114,000	$2,771	$33,258
$940	$92,800	$747	$116,000	$2,820	$33,841
$956	$94,400	$760	$118,000	$2,869	$34,425
$972	$96,000	$772	$120,000	$2,917	$35,008
$989	$97,600	$785	$122,000	$2,966	$35,592
$1,005	$99,200	$798	$124,000	$3,015	$36,175
$1,021	$100,800	$811	$126,000	$3,063	$36,759
$1,037	$102,400	$824	$128,000	$3,112	$37,342
$1,053	$104,000	$837	$130,000	$3,160	$37,926
$1,070	$105,600	$850	$132,000	$3,209	$38,509
$1,086	$107,200	$863	$134,000	$3,258	$39,093

Monthly payment	Maximum mortgage		Maximum price	Income to qualify	
	Amount	P & I		Monthly	Annual
$1,102	$108,800	$875	$136,000	$3,306	$39,676
$1,118	$110,400	$888	$138,000	$3,355	$40,260
$1,135	$112,000	$901	$140,000	$3,404	$40,843
$1,151	$113,600	$914	$142,000	$3,452	$41,427
$1,167	$115,200	$927	$144,000	$3,501	$42,010
$1,183	$116,800	$940	$146,000	$3,549	$42,594
$1,199	$118,400	$953	$148,000	$3,598	$43,177
$1,216	$120,000	$966	$150,000	$3,647	$43,760
$1,232	$121,600	$978	$152,000	$3,695	$44,344
$1,248	$123,200	$991	$154,000	$3,744	$44,927
$1,264	$124,800	$1,004	$156,000	$3,793	$45,511
$1,280	$126,400	$1,017	$158,000	$3,841	$46,094
$1,297	$128,000	$1,030	$160,000	$3,890	$46,678
$1,313	$129,600	$1,043	$162,000	$3,938	$47,261
$1,329	$131,200	$1,056	$164,000	$3,987	$47,845
$1,345	$132,800	$1,069	$166,000	$4,036	$48,428
$1,361	$134,400	$1,081	$168,000	$4,084	$49,012
$1,378	$136,000	$1,094	$170,000	$4,133	$49,595
$1,394	$137,600	$1,107	$172,000	$4,182	$50,179
$1,410	$139,200	$1,120	$174,000	$4,230	$50,762
$1,426	$140,800	$1,133	$176,000	$4,279	$51,346
$1,442	$142,400	$1,146	$178,000	$4,327	$51,929
$1,459	$144,000	$1,159	$180,000	$4,376	$52,513
$1,475	$145,600	$1,172	$182,000	$4,425	$53,096
$1,491	$147,200	$1,184	$184,000	$4,473	$53,679
$1,507	$148,800	$1,197	$186,000	$4,522	$54,263
$1,524	$150,400	$1,210	$188,000	$4,571	$54,846
$1,540	$152,000	$1,223	$190,000	$4,619	$55,430
$1,556	$153,600	$1,236	$192,000	$4,668	$56,013
$1,572	$155,200	$1,249	$194,000	$4,716	$56,597
$1,588	$156,800	$1,262	$196,000	$4,765	$57,180
$1,605	$158,400	$1,275	$198,000	$4,814	$57,764
$1,621	$160,000	$1,287	$200,000	$4,862	$58,347

9½% Interest, 30-Year Term, 20% Down

(2% of purchase price assumed for taxes and insurance; 33% of gross monthly income allowed for mortgage payment)

Monthly payment	Maximum mortgage		Maximum price	Income to qualify	
	Amount	P & I		Monthly	Annual
$420	$40,000	$336	$50,000	$1,259	$15,109
$436	$41,600	$350	$52,000	$1,309	$15,713
$453	$43,200	$363	$54,000	$1,360	$16,317
$470	$44,800	$377	$56,000	$1,410	$16,922
$487	$46,400	$390	$58,000	$1,460	$17,526
$504	$48,000	$404	$60,000	$1,511	$18,130
$520	$49,600	$417	$62,000	$1,561	$18,735
$537	$51,200	$431	$64,000	$1,612	$19,339
$554	$52,800	$444	$66,000	$1,662	$19,943
$571	$54,400	$457	$68,000	$1,712	$20,548
$588	$56,000	$471	$70,000	$1,763	$21,152
$604	$57,600	$484	$72,000	$1,813	$21,756
$621	$59,200	$498	$74,000	$1,863	$22,361
$638	$60,800	$511	$76,000	$1,914	$22,965
$655	$62,400	$525	$78,000	$1,964	$23,569
$671	$64,000	$538	$80,000	$2,014	$24,174
$688	$65,600	$552	$82,000	$2,065	$24,778
$705	$67,200	$565	$84,000	$2,115	$25,382
$722	$68,800	$579	$86,000	$2,166	$25,987
$739	$70,400	$592	$88,000	$2,216	$26,591
$755	$72,000	$605	$90,000	$2,266	$27,195
$772	$73,600	$619	$92,000	$2,317	$27,800
$789	$75,200	$632	$94,000	$2,367	$28,404
$806	$76,800	$646	$96,000	$2,417	$29,008
$823	$78,400	$659	$98,000	$2,468	$29,613
$839	$80,000	$673	$100,000	$2,518	$30,217
$856	$81,600	$686	$102,000	$2,568	$30,821
$873	$83,200	$700	$104,000	$2,619	$31,426
$890	$84,800	$713	$106,000	$2,669	$32,030
$907	$86,400	$727	$108,000	$2,720	$32,634
$923	$88,000	$740	$110,000	$2,770	$33,239
$940	$89,600	$753	$112,000	$2,820	$33,843
$957	$91,200	$767	$114,000	$2,871	$34,447
$974	$92,800	$780	$116,000	$2,921	$35,052
$990	$94,400	$794	$118,000	$2,971	$35,656
$1,007	$96,000	$807	$120,000	$3,022	$36,260
$1,024	$97,600	$821	$122,000	$3,072	$36,865
$1,041	$99,200	$834	$124,000	$3,122	$37,469
$1,058	$100,800	$848	$126,000	$3,173	$38,073
$1,074	$102,400	$861	$128,000	$3,223	$38,678
$1,091	$104,000	$875	$130,000	$3,274	$39,282
$1,108	$105,600	$888	$132,000	$3,324	$39,887
$1,125	$107,200	$901	$134,000	$3,374	$40,491

Monthly payment	Maximum mortgage		Maximum price	Income to qualify	
	Amount	P & I		Monthly	Annual
$1,142	$108,800	$915	$136,000	$3,425	$41,095
$1,158	$110,400	$928	$138,000	$3,475	$41,700
$1,175	$112,000	$942	$140,000	$3,525	$42,304
$1,192	$113,600	$955	$142,000	$3,576	$42,908
$1,209	$115,200	$969	$144,000	$3,626	$43,513
$1,225	$116,800	$982	$146,000	$3,676	$44,117
$1,242	$118,400	$996	$148,000	$3,727	$44,721
$1,259	$120,000	$1,009	$150,000	$3,777	$45,326
$1,276	$121,600	$1,022	$152,000	$3,827	$45,930
$1,293	$123,200	$1,036	$154,000	$3,878	$46,534
$1,309	$124,800	$1,049	$156,000	$3,928	$47,139
$1,326	$126,400	$1,063	$158,000	$3,979	$47,743
$1,343	$128,000	$1,076	$160,000	$4,029	$48,347
$1,360	$129,600	$1,090	$162,000	$4,079	$48,952
$1,377	$131,200	$1,103	$164,000	$4,130	$49,556
$1,393	$132,800	$1,117	$166,000	$4,180	$50,160
$1,410	$134,400	$1,130	$168,000	$4,230	$50,765
$1,427	$136,000	$1,144	$170,000	$4,281	$51,369
$1,444	$137,600	$1,157	$172,000	$4,331	$51,973
$1,460	$139,200	$1,170	$174,000	$4,381	$52,578
$1,477	$140,800	$1,184	$176,000	$4,432	$53,182
$1,494	$142,400	$1,197	$178,000	$4,482	$53,786
$1,511	$144,000	$1,211	$180,000	$4,533	$54,391
$1,528	$145,600	$1,224	$182,000	$4,583	$54,995
$1,544	$147,200	$1,238	$184,000	$4,633	$55,599
$1,561	$148,800	$1,251	$186,000	$4,684	$56,204
$1,578	$150,400	$1,265	$188,000	$4,734	$56,808
$1,595	$152,000	$1,278	$190,000	$4,784	$57,412
$1,612	$153,600	$1,292	$192,000	$4,835	$58,017
$1,628	$155,200	$1,305	$194,000	$4,885	$58,621
$1,645	$156,800	$1,318	$196,000	$4,935	$59,225
$1,662	$158,400	$1,332	$198,000	$4,986	$59,830
$1,679	$160,000	$1,345	$200,000	$5,036	$60,434

10% Interest, 30-Year Term, 20% Down

(2% of purchase price assumed for taxes and insurance; 33% of gross monthly income allowed for mortgage payment)

Monthly payment	Maximum mortgage		Maximum price	Income to qualify	
	Amount	P & I		Monthly	Annual
$434	$40,000	$351	$50,000	$1,303	$15,637
$452	$41,600	$365	$52,000	$1,355	$16,263
$469	$43,200	$379	$54,000	$1,407	$16,888
$486	$44,800	$393	$56,000	$1,459	$17,514
$504	$46,400	$407	$58,000	$1,512	$18,139
$521	$48,000	$421	$60,000	$1,564	$18,765
$539	$49,600	$435	$62,000	$1,616	$19,390
$556	$51,200	$449	$64,000	$1,668	$20,016
$573	$52,800	$463	$66,000	$1,720	$20,641
$591	$54,400	$477	$68,000	$1,772	$21,267
$608	$56,000	$491	$70,000	$1,824	$21,892
$625	$57,600	$505	$72,000	$1,876	$22,517
$643	$59,200	$520	$74,000	$1,929	$23,143
$660	$60,800	$534	$76,000	$1,981	$23,768
$678	$62,400	$548	$78,000	$2,033	$24,394
$695	$64,000	$562	$80,000	$2,085	$25,019
$712	$65,600	$576	$82,000	$2,137	$25,645
$730	$67,200	$590	$84,000	$2,189	$26,270
$747	$68,800	$604	$86,000	$2,241	$26,896
$764	$70,400	$618	$88,000	$2,293	$27,521
$782	$72,000	$632	$90,000	$2,346	$28,147
$799	$73,600	$646	$92,000	$2,398	$28,772
$817	$75,200	$660	$94,000	$2,450	$29,398
$834	$76,800	$674	$96,000	$2,502	$30,023
$851	$78,400	$688	$98,000	$2,554	$30,649
$869	$80,000	$702	$100,000	$2,606	$31,274
$886	$81,600	$716	$102,000	$2,658	$31,900
$903	$83,200	$730	$104,000	$2,710	$32,525
$921	$84,800	$744	$106,000	$2,763	$33,151
$938	$86,400	$758	$108,000	$2,815	$33,776
$956	$88,000	$772	$110,000	$2,867	$34,402
$973	$89,600	$786	$112,000	$2,919	$35,027
$990	$91,200	$800	$114,000	$2,971	$35,653
$1,008	$92,800	$814	$116,000	$3,023	$36,278
$1,025	$94,400	$828	$118,000	$3,075	$36,904
$1,042	$96,000	$842	$120,000	$3,127	$37,529
$1,060	$97,600	$857	$122,000	$3,180	$38,155
$1,077	$99,200	$871	$124,000	$3,232	$38,780
$1,095	$100,800	$885	$126,000	$3,284	$39,406
$1,112	$102,400	$899	$128,000	$3,336	$40,031
$1,129	$104,000	$913	$130,000	$3,388	$40,657
$1,147	$105,600	$927	$132,000	$3,440	$41,282
$1,164	$107,200	$941	$134,000	$3,492	$41,908

Monthly payment	Maximum mortgage		Maximum price	Income to qualify	
	Amount	P & I		Monthly	Annual
$1,181	$108,800	$955	$136,000	$3,544	$42,533
$1,199	$110,400	$969	$138,000	$3,597	$43,159
$1,216	$112,000	$983	$140,000	$3,649	$43,784
$1,234	$113,600	$997	$142,000	$3,701	$44,410
$1,251	$115,200	$1,011	$144,000	$3,753	$45,035
$1,268	$116,800	$1,025	$146,000	$3,805	$45,660
$1,286	$118,400	$1,039	$148,000	$3,857	$46,286
$1,303	$120,000	$1,053	$150,000	$3,909	$46,911
$1,320	$121,600	$1,067	$152,000	$3,961	$47,537
$1,338	$123,200	$1,081	$154,000	$4,014	$48,162
$1,355	$124,800	$1,095	$156,000	$4,066	$48,788
$1,373	$126,400	$1,109	$158,000	$4,118	$49,413
$1,390	$128,000	$1,123	$160,000	$4,170	$50,039
$1,407	$129,600	$1,137	$162,000	$4,222	$50,664
$1,425	$131,200	$1,151	$164,000	$4,274	$51,290
$1,442	$132,800	$1,165	$166,000	$4,326	$51,915
$1,459	$134,400	$1,179	$168,000	$4,378	$52,541
$1,477	$136,000	$1,194	$170,000	$4,431	$53,166
$1,494	$137,600	$1,208	$172,000	$4,483	$53,792
$1,512	$139,200	$1,222	$174,000	$4,535	$54,417
$1,529	$140,800	$1,236	$176,000	$4,587	$55,043
$1,546	$142,400	$1,250	$178,000	$4,639	$55,668
$1,564	$144,000	$1,264	$180,000	$4,691	$56,294
$1,581	$145,600	$1,278	$182,000	$4,743	$56,919
$1,598	$147,200	$1,292	$184,000	$4,795	$57,545
$1,616	$148,800	$1,306	$186,000	$4,848	$58,170
$1,633	$150,400	$1,320	$188,000	$4,900	$58,796
$1,651	$152,000	$1,334	$190,000	$4,952	$59,421
$1,668	$153,600	$1,348	$192,000	$5,004	$60,047
$1,685	$155,200	$1,362	$194,000	$5,056	$60,672
$1,703	$156,800	$1,376	$196,000	$5,108	$61,298
$1,720	$158,400	$1,390	$198,000	$5,160	$61,923
$1,737	$160,000	$1,404	$200,000	$5,212	$62,549

10½% Interest, 30-Year Term, 20% Down

(2% of purchase price assumed for taxes and insurance; 33% of gross monthly income allowed for mortgage payment)

Monthly payment	Maximum mortgage		Maximum price	Income to qualify	
	Amount	P & I		Monthly	Annual
$449	$40,000	$366	$50,000	$1,348	$16,172
$467	$41,600	$381	$52,000	$1,402	$16,819
$485	$43,200	$395	$54,000	$1,456	$17,466
$503	$44,800	$410	$56,000	$1,509	$18,113
$521	$46,400	$424	$58,000	$1,563	$18,760
$539	$48,000	$439	$60,000	$1,617	$19,407
$557	$49,600	$454	$62,000	$1,671	$20,054
$575	$51,200	$468	$64,000	$1,725	$20,701
$593	$52,800	$483	$66,000	$1,779	$21,348
$611	$54,400	$498	$68,000	$1,833	$21,994
$629	$56,000	$512	$70,000	$1,887	$22,641
$647	$57,600	$527	$72,000	$1,941	$23,288
$665	$59,200	$542	$74,000	$1,995	$23,935
$683	$60,800	$556	$76,000	$2,049	$24,582
$701	$62,400	$571	$78,000	$2,102	$25,229
$719	$64,000	$585	$80,000	$2,156	$25,876
$737	$65,600	$600	$82,000	$2,210	$26,523
$755	$67,200	$615	$84,000	$2,264	$27,170
$773	$68,800	$629	$86,000	$2,318	$27,817
$791	$70,400	$644	$88,000	$2,372	$28,463
$809	$72,000	$659	$90,000	$2,426	$29,110
$827	$73,600	$673	$92,000	$2,480	$29,757
$845	$75,200	$688	$94,000	$2,534	$30,404
$863	$76,800	$703	$96,000	$2,588	$31,051
$880	$78,400	$717	$98,000	$2,641	$31,698
$898	$80,000	$732	$100,000	$2,695	$32,345
$916	$81,600	$746	$102,000	$2,749	$32,992
$934	$83,200	$761	$104,000	$2,803	$33,639
$952	$84,800	$776	$106,000	$2,857	$34,285
$970	$86,400	$790	$108,000	$2,911	$34,932
$988	$88,000	$805	$110,000	$2,965	$35,579
$1,006	$89,600	$820	$112,000	$3,019	$36,226
$1,024	$91,200	$834	$114,000	$3,073	$36,873
$1,042	$92,800	$849	$116,000	$3,127	$37,520
$1,060	$94,400	$864	$118,000	$3,181	$38,167
$1,078	$96,000	$878	$120,000	$3,234	$38,814
$1,096	$97,600	$893	$122,000	$3,288	$39,461
$1,114	$99,200	$907	$124,000	$3,342	$40,108
$1,132	$100,800	$922	$126,000	$3,396	$40,754
$1,150	$102,400	$937	$128,000	$3,450	$41,401
$1,168	$104,000	$951	$130,000	$3,504	$42,048
$1,186	$105,600	$966	$132,000	$3,558	$42,695
$1,204	$107,200	$981	$134,000	$3,612	$43,342

Monthly payment	Maximum mortgage		Maximum price	Income to qualify	
	Amount	P & I		Monthly	Annual
$1,222	$108,800	$995	$136,000	$3,666	$43,989
$1,240	$110,400	$1,010	$138,000	$3,720	$44,636
$1,258	$112,000	$1,025	$140,000	$3,774	$45,283
$1,276	$113,600	$1,039	$142,000	$3,827	$45,930
$1,294	$115,200	$1,054	$144,000	$3,881	$46,577
$1,312	$116,800	$1,068	$146,000	$3,935	$47,223
$1,330	$118,400	$1,083	$148,000	$3,989	$47,870
$1,348	$120,000	$1,098	$150,000	$4,043	$48,517
$1,366	$121,600	$1,112	$152,000	$4,097	$49,164
$1,384	$123,200	$1,127	$154,000	$4,151	$49,811
$1,402	$124,800	$1,142	$156,000	$4,205	$50,458
$1,420	$126,400	$1,156	$158,000	$4,259	$51,105
$1,438	$128,000	$1,171	$160,000	$4,313	$51,752
$1,456	$129,600	$1,186	$162,000	$4,367	$52,399
$1,473	$131,200	$1,200	$164,000	$4,420	$53,045
$1,491	$132,800	$1,215	$166,000	$4,474	$53,692
$1,509	$134,400	$1,229	$168,000	$4,528	$54,339
$1,527	$136,000	$1,244	$170,000	$4,582	$54,986
$1,545	$137,600	$1,259	$172,000	$4,636	$55,633
$1,563	$139,200	$1,273	$174,000	$4,690	$56,280
$1,581	$140,800	$1,288	$176,000	$4,744	$56,927
$1,599	$142,400	$1,303	$178,000	$4,798	$57,574
$1,617	$144,000	$1,317	$180,000	$4,852	$58,221
$1,635	$145,600	$1,332	$182,000	$4,906	$58,868
$1,653	$147,200	$1,347	$184,000	$4,960	$59,514
$1,671	$148,800	$1,361	$186,000	$5,013	$60,161
$1,689	$150,400	$1,376	$188,000	$5,067	$60,808
$1,707	$152,000	$1,390	$190,000	$5,121	$61,455
$1,725	$153,600	$1,405	$192,000	$5,175	$62,102
$1,743	$155,200	$1,420	$194,000	$5,229	$62,749
$1,761	$156,800	$1,434	$196,000	$5,283	$63,396
$1,779	$158,400	$1,449	$198,000	$5,337	$64,043
$1,797	$160,000	$1,464	$200,000	$5,391	$64,690

11% Interest, 30-Year Term, 20% Down

(2% of purchase price assumed for taxes and insurance; 33% of gross monthly income allowed for mortgage payment)

Monthly payment	Maximum mortgage		Maximum price	Income to qualify	
	Amount	P & I		Monthly	Annual
$464	$40,000	$381	$50,000	$1,393	$16,714
$483	$41,600	$396	$52,000	$1,449	$17,382
$501	$43,200	$411	$54,000	$1,504	$18,051
$520	$44,800	$427	$56,000	$1,560	$18,719
$539	$46,400	$442	$58,000	$1,616	$19,388
$557	$48,000	$457	$60,000	$1,671	$20,056
$576	$49,600	$472	$62,000	$1,727	$20,725
$594	$51,200	$488	$64,000	$1,783	$21,394
$613	$52,800	$503	$66,000	$1,839	$22,062
$631	$54,400	$518	$68,000	$1,894	$22,731
$650	$56,000	$533	$70,000	$1,950	$23,399
$669	$57,600	$549	$72,000	$2,006	$24,068
$687	$59,200	$564	$74,000	$2,061	$24,736
$706	$60,800	$579	$76,000	$2,117	$25,405
$724	$62,400	$594	$78,000	$2,173	$26,073
$743	$64,000	$609	$80,000	$2,228	$26,742
$761	$65,600	$625	$82,000	$2,284	$27,410
$780	$67,200	$640	$84,000	$2,340	$28,079
$799	$68,800	$655	$86,000	$2,396	$28,748
$817	$70,400	$670	$88,000	$2,451	$29,416
$836	$72,000	$686	$90,000	$2,507	$30,085
$854	$73,600	$701	$92,000	$2,563	$30,753
$873	$75,200	$716	$94,000	$2,618	$31,422
$891	$76,800	$731	$96,000	$2,674	$32,090
$910	$78,400	$747	$98,000	$2,730	$32,759
$929	$80,000	$762	$100,000	$2,786	$33,427
$947	$81,600	$777	$102,000	$2,841	$34,096
$966	$83,200	$792	$104,000	$2,897	$34,764
$984	$84,800	$808	$106,000	$2,953	$35,433
$1,003	$86,400	$823	$108,000	$3,008	$36,102
$1,021	$88,000	$838	$110,000	$3,064	$36,770
$1,040	$89,600	$853	$112,000	$3,120	$37,439
$1,059	$91,200	$869	$114,000	$3,176	$38,107
$1,077	$92,800	$884	$116,000	$3,231	$38,776
$1,096	$94,400	$899	$118,000	$3,287	$39,444
$1,114	$96,000	$914	$120,000	$3,343	$40,113
$1,133	$97,600	$929	$122,000	$3,398	$40,781
$1,151	$99,200	$945	$124,000	$3,454	$41,450
$1,170	$100,800	$960	$126,000	$3,510	$42,119
$1,189	$102,400	$975	$128,000	$3,566	$42,787
$1,207	$104,000	$990	$130,000	$3,621	$43,456
$1,226	$105,600	$1,006	$132,000	$3,677	$44,124
$1,244	$107,200	$1,021	$134,000	$3,733	$44,793

Monthly payment	Maximum mortgage		Maximum price	Income to qualify	
	Amount	P & I		Monthly	Annual
$1,263	$108,800	$1,036	$136,000	$3,788	$45,461
$1,281	$110,400	$1,051	$138,000	$3,844	$46,130
$1,300	$112,000	$1,067	$140,000	$3,900	$46,798
$1,319	$113,600	$1,082	$142,000	$3,956	$47,467
$1,337	$115,200	$1,097	$144,000	$4,011	$48,135
$1,356	$116,800	$1,112	$146,000	$4,067	$48,804
$1,374	$118,400	$1,128	$148,000	$4,123	$49,473
$1,393	$120,000	$1,143	$150,000	$4,178	$50,141
$1,411	$121,600	$1,158	$152,000	$4,234	$50,810
$1,430	$123,200	$1,173	$154,000	$4,290	$51,478
$1,449	$124,800	$1,189	$156,000	$4,346	$52,147
$1,467	$126,400	$1,204	$158,000	$4,401	$52,815
$1,486	$128,000	$1,219	$160,000	$4,457	$53,484
$1,504	$129,600	$1,234	$162,000	$4,513	$54,152
$1,523	$131,200	$1,249	$164,000	$4,568	$54,821
$1,541	$132,800	$1,265	$166,000	$4,624	$55,489
$1,560	$134,400	$1,280	$168,000	$4,680	$56,158
$1,579	$136,000	$1,295	$170,000	$4,736	$56,827
$1,597	$137,600	$1,310	$172,000	$4,791	$57,495
$1,616	$139,200	$1,326	$174,000	$4,847	$58,164
$1,634	$140,800	$1,341	$176,000	$4,903	$58,832
$1,653	$142,400	$1,356	$178,000	$4,958	$59,501
$1,671	$144,000	$1,371	$180,000	$5,014	$60,169
$1,690	$145,600	$1,387	$182,000	$5,070	$60,838
$1,709	$147,200	$1,402	$184,000	$5,126	$61,506
$1,727	$148,800	$1,417	$186,000	$5,181	$62,175
$1,746	$150,400	$1,432	$188,000	$5,237	$62,843
$1,764	$152,000	$1,448	$190,000	$5,293	$63,512
$1,783	$153,600	$1,463	$192,000	$5,348	$64,181
$1,801	$155,200	$1,478	$194,000	$5,404	$64,849
$1,820	$156,800	$1,493	$196,000	$5,460	$65,518
$1,839	$158,400	$1,509	$198,000	$5,516	$66,186
$1,857	$160,000	$1,524	$200,000	$5,571	$66,855

11½% Interest, 30-Year Term, 20% Down

(2% of purchase price assumed for taxes and insurance; 33% of gross monthly income allowed for mortgage payment)

Monthly payment	Maximum mortgage		Maximum price	Income to qualify	
	Amount	P & I		Monthly	Annual
$479	$40,000	$396	$50,000	$1,438	$17,260
$499	$41,600	$412	$52,000	$1,496	$17,951
$518	$43,200	$428	$54,000	$1,553	$18,641
$537	$44,800	$444	$56,000	$1,611	$19,332
$556	$46,400	$459	$58,000	$1,668	$20,022
$575	$48,000	$475	$60,000	$1,726	$20,712
$595	$49,600	$491	$62,000	$1,784	$21,403
$614	$51,200	$507	$64,000	$1,841	$22,093
$633	$52,800	$523	$66,000	$1,899	$22,784
$652	$54,400	$539	$68,000	$1,956	$23,474
$671	$56,000	$555	$70,000	$2,014	$24,164
$690	$57,600	$570	$72,000	$2,071	$24,855
$710	$59,200	$586	$74,000	$2,129	$25,545
$729	$60,800	$602	$76,000	$2,186	$26,236
$748	$62,400	$618	$78,000	$2,244	$26,926
$767	$64,000	$634	$80,000	$2,301	$27,617
$786	$65,600	$650	$82,000	$2,359	$28,307
$805	$67,200	$665	$84,000	$2,416	$28,997
$825	$68,800	$681	$86,000	$2,474	$29,688
$844	$70,400	$697	$88,000	$2,532	$30,378
$863	$72,000	$713	$90,000	$2,589	$31,069
$882	$73,600	$729	$92,000	$2,647	$31,759
$901	$75,200	$745	$94,000	$2,704	$32,449
$921	$76,800	$761	$96,000	$2,762	$33,140
$940	$78,400	$776	$98,000	$2,819	$33,830
$959	$80,000	$792	$100,000	$2,877	$34,521
$978	$81,600	$808	$102,000	$2,934	$35,211
$997	$83,200	$824	$104,000	$2,992	$35,901
$1,016	$84,800	$840	$106,000	$3,049	$36,592
$1,036	$86,400	$856	$108,000	$3,107	$37,282
$1,055	$88,000	$871	$110,000	$3,164	$37,973
$1,074	$89,600	$887	$112,000	$3,222	$38,663
$1,093	$91,200	$903	$114,000	$3,279	$39,354
$1,112	$92,800	$919	$116,000	$3,337	$40,044
$1,132	$94,400	$935	$118,000	$3,395	$40,734
$1,151	$96,000	$951	$120,000	$3,452	$41,425
$1,170	$97,600	$967	$122,000	$3,510	$42,115
$1,189	$99,200	$982	$124,000	$3,567	$42,806
$1,208	$100,800	$998	$126,000	$3,625	$43,496
$1,227	$102,400	$1,014	$128,000	$3,682	$44,186
$1,247	$104,000	$1,030	$130,000	$3,740	$44,877
$1,266	$105,600	$1,046	$132,000	$3,797	$45,567
$1,285	$107,200	$1,062	$134,000	$3,855	$46,258

Monthly payment	Maximum mortgage		Maximum price	Income to qualify	
	Amount	P & I		Monthly	Annual
$1,304	$108,800	$1,077	$136,000	$3,912	$46,948
$1,323	$110,400	$1,093	$138,000	$3,970	$47,638
$1,342	$112,000	$1,109	$140,000	$4,027	$48,329
$1,362	$113,600	$1,125	$142,000	$4,085	$49,019
$1,381	$115,200	$1,141	$144,000	$4,142	$49,710
$1,400	$116,800	$1,157	$146,000	$4,200	$50,400
$1,419	$118,400	$1,173	$148,000	$4,258	$51,091
$1,438	$120,000	$1,188	$150,000	$4,315	$51,781
$1,458	$121,600	$1,204	$152,000	$4,373	$52,471
$1,477	$123,200	$1,220	$154,000	$4,430	$53,162
$1,496	$124,800	$1,236	$156,000	$4,488	$53,852
$1,515	$126,400	$1,252	$158,000	$4,545	$54,543
$1,534	$128,000	$1,268	$160,000	$4,603	$55,233
$1,553	$129,600	$1,283	$162,000	$4,660	$55,923
$1,573	$131,200	$1,299	$164,000	$4,718	$56,614
$1,592	$132,800	$1,315	$166,000	$4,775	$57,304
$1,611	$134,400	$1,331	$168,000	$4,833	$57,995
$1,630	$136,000	$1,347	$170,000	$4,890	$58,685
$1,649	$137,600	$1,363	$172,000	$4,948	$59,376
$1,668	$139,200	$1,378	$174,000	$5,005	$60,066
$1,688	$140,800	$1,394	$176,000	$5,063	$60,756
$1,707	$142,400	$1,410	$178,000	$5,121	$61,447
$1,726	$144,000	$1,426	$180,000	$5,178	$62,137
$1,745	$145,600	$1,442	$182,000	$5,236	$62,828
$1,764	$147,200	$1,458	$184,000	$5,293	$63,518
$1,784	$148,800	$1,474	$186,000	$5,351	$64,208
$1,803	$150,400	$1,489	$188,000	$5,408	$64,899
$1,822	$152,000	$1,505	$190,000	$5,466	$65,589
$1,841	$153,600	$1,521	$192,000	$5,523	$66,280
$1,860	$155,200	$1,537	$194,000	$5,581	$66,970
$1,879	$156,800	$1,553	$196,000	$5,638	$67,660
$1,899	$158,400	$1,569	$198,000	$5,696	$68,351
$1,918	$160,000	$1,584	$200,000	$5,753	$69,041

12% Interest, 30-Year Term, 20% Down

(2% of purchase price assumed for taxes and insurance; 33% of gross monthly income allowed for mortgage payment)

Monthly payment	Maximum mortgage Amount	Maximum mortgage P & I	Maximum price	Income to qualify Monthly	Income to qualify Annual
$495	$40,000	$411	$50,000	$1,484	$17,812
$515	$41,600	$428	$52,000	$1,544	$18,525
$534	$43,200	$444	$54,000	$1,603	$19,237
$554	$44,800	$461	$56,000	$1,662	$19,950
$574	$46,400	$477	$58,000	$1,722	$20,662
$594	$48,000	$494	$60,000	$1,781	$21,375
$614	$49,600	$510	$62,000	$1,841	$22,087
$633	$51,200	$527	$64,000	$1,900	$22,800
$653	$52,800	$543	$66,000	$1,959	$23,512
$673	$54,400	$560	$68,000	$2,019	$24,225
$693	$56,000	$576	$70,000	$2,078	$24,937
$712	$57,600	$592	$72,000	$2,137	$25,650
$732	$59,200	$609	$74,000	$2,197	$26,362
$752	$60,800	$625	$76,000	$2,256	$27,075
$772	$62,400	$642	$78,000	$2,316	$27,787
$792	$64,000	$658	$80,000	$2,375	$28,500
$811	$65,600	$675	$82,000	$2,434	$29,212
$831	$67,200	$691	$84,000	$2,494	$29,925
$851	$68,800	$708	$86,000	$2,553	$30,637
$871	$70,400	$724	$88,000	$2,612	$31,350
$891	$72,000	$741	$90,000	$2,672	$32,062
$910	$73,600	$757	$92,000	$2,731	$32,775
$930	$75,200	$774	$94,000	$2,791	$33,487
$950	$76,800	$790	$96,000	$2,850	$34,200
$970	$78,400	$806	$98,000	$2,909	$34,912
$990	$80,000	$823	$100,000	$2,969	$35,625
$1,009	$81,600	$839	$102,000	$3,028	$36,337
$1,029	$83,200	$856	$104,000	$3,087	$37,050
$1,049	$84,800	$872	$106,000	$3,147	$37,762
$1,069	$86,400	$889	$108,000	$3,206	$38,475
$1,089	$88,000	$905	$110,000	$3,266	$39,187
$1,108	$89,600	$922	$112,000	$3,325	$39,899
$1,128	$91,200	$938	$114,000	$3,384	$40,612
$1,148	$92,800	$955	$116,000	$3,444	$41,324
$1,168	$94,400	$971	$118,000	$3,503	$42,037
$1,187	$96,000	$987	$120,000	$3,562	$42,749
$1,207	$97,600	$1,004	$122,000	$3,622	$43,462
$1,227	$99,200	$1,020	$124,000	$3,681	$44,174
$1,247	$100,800	$1,037	$126,000	$3,741	$44,887
$1,267	$102,400	$1,053	$128,000	$3,800	$45,599
$1,286	$104,000	$1,070	$130,000	$3,859	$46,312
$1,306	$105,600	$1,086	$132,000	$3,919	$47,024
$1,326	$107,200	$1,103	$134,000	$3,978	$47,737

Monthly payment	Maximum mortgage		Maximum price	Income to qualify	
	Amount	P & I		Monthly	Annual
$1,346	$108,800	$1,119	$136,000	$4,037	$48,449
$1,366	$110,400	$1,136	$138,000	$4,097	$49,162
$1,385	$112,000	$1,152	$140,000	$4,156	$49,874
$1,405	$113,600	$1,169	$142,000	$4,216	$50,587
$1,425	$115,200	$1,185	$144,000	$4,275	$51,299
$1,445	$116,800	$1,201	$146,000	$4,334	$52,012
$1,465	$118,400	$1,218	$148,000	$4,394	$52,724
$1,484	$120,000	$1,234	$150,000	$4,453	$53,437
$1,504	$121,600	$1,251	$152,000	$4,512	$54,149
$1,524	$123,200	$1,267	$154,000	$4,572	$54,862
$1,544	$124,800	$1,284	$156,000	$4,631	$55,574
$1,564	$126,400	$1,300	$158,000	$4,691	$56,287
$1,583	$128,000	$1,317	$160,000	$4,750	$56,999
$1,603	$129,600	$1,333	$162,000	$4,809	$57,712
$1,623	$131,200	$1,350	$164,000	$4,869	$58,424
$1,643	$132,800	$1,366	$166,000	$4,928	$59,137
$1,662	$134,400	$1,382	$168,000	$4,987	$59,849
$1,682	$136,000	$1,399	$170,000	$5,047	$60,562
$1,702	$137,600	$1,415	$172,000	$5,106	$61,274
$1,722	$139,200	$1,432	$174,000	$5,166	$61,987
$1,742	$140,800	$1,448	$176,000	$5,225	$62,699
$1,761	$142,400	$1,465	$178,000	$5,284	$63,412
$1,781	$144,000	$1,481	$180,000	$5,344	$64,124
$1,801	$145,600	$1,498	$182,000	$5,403	$64,837
$1,821	$147,200	$1,514	$184,000	$5,462	$65,549
$1,841	$148,800	$1,531	$186,000	$5,522	$66,262
$1,860	$150,400	$1,547	$188,000	$5,581	$66,974
$1,880	$152,000	$1,564	$190,000	$5,641	$67,687
$1,900	$153,600	$1,580	$192,000	$5,700	$68,399
$1,920	$155,200	$1,596	$194,000	$5,759	$69,112
$1,940	$156,800	$1,613	$196,000	$5,819	$69,824
$1,959	$158,400	$1,629	$198,000	$5,878	$70,537
$1,979	$160,000	$1,646	$200,000	$5,937	$71,249

12½% Interest, 30-Year Term, 20% Down

(2% of purchase price assumed for taxes and insurance; 33% of gross monthly income allowed for mortgage payment)

Monthly payment	Maximum mortgage Amount	Maximum mortgage P & I	Maximum price	Income to qualify Monthly	Income to qualify Annual
$510	$40,000	$427	$50,000	$1,531	$18,369
$531	$41,600	$444	$52,000	$1,592	$19,103
$551	$43,200	$461	$54,000	$1,653	$19,838
$571	$44,800	$478	$56,000	$1,714	$20,573
$592	$46,400	$495	$58,000	$1,776	$21,308
$612	$48,000	$512	$60,000	$1,837	$22,042
$633	$49,600	$529	$62,000	$1,898	$22,777
$653	$51,200	$546	$64,000	$1,959	$23,512
$674	$52,800	$564	$66,000	$2,021	$24,247
$694	$54,400	$581	$68,000	$2,082	$24,981
$714	$56,000	$598	$70,000	$2,143	$25,716
$735	$57,600	$615	$72,000	$2,204	$26,451
$755	$59,200	$632	$74,000	$2,265	$27,186
$776	$60,800	$649	$76,000	$2,327	$27,920
$796	$62,400	$666	$78,000	$2,388	$28,655
$816	$64,000	$683	$80,000	$2,449	$29,390
$837	$65,600	$700	$82,000	$2,510	$30,125
$857	$67,200	$717	$84,000	$2,572	$30,859
$878	$68,800	$734	$86,000	$2,633	$31,594
$898	$70,400	$751	$88,000	$2,694	$32,329
$918	$72,000	$768	$90,000	$2,755	$33,064
$939	$73,600	$786	$92,000	$2,817	$33,798
$959	$75,200	$803	$94,000	$2,878	$34,533
$980	$76,800	$820	$96,000	$2,939	$35,268
$1,000	$78,400	$837	$98,000	$3,000	$36,003
$1,020	$80,000	$854	$100,000	$3,061	$36,737
$1,041	$81,600	$871	$102,000	$3,123	$37,472
$1,061	$83,200	$888	$104,000	$3,184	$38,207
$1,082	$84,800	$905	$106,000	$3,245	$38,942
$1,102	$86,400	$922	$108,000	$3,306	$39,676
$1,123	$88,000	$939	$110,000	$3,368	$40,411
$1,143	$89,600	$956	$112,000	$3,429	$41,146
$1,163	$91,200	$973	$114,000	$3,490	$41,881
$1,184	$92,800	$990	$116,000	$3,551	$42,615
$1,204	$94,400	$1,008	$118,000	$3,613	$43,350
$1,225	$96,000	$1,025	$120,000	$3,674	$44,085
$1,245	$97,600	$1,042	$122,000	$3,735	$44,820
$1,265	$99,200	$1,059	$124,000	$3,796	$45,554
$1,286	$100,800	$1,076	$126,000	$3,857	$46,289
$1,306	$102,400	$1,093	$128,000	$3,919	$47,024
$1,327	$104,000	$1,110	$130,000	$3,980	$47,759
$1,347	$105,600	$1,127	$132,000	$4,041	$48,493
$1,367	$107,200	$1,144	$134,000	$4,102	$49,228

Monthly payment	Maximum mortgage		Maximum price	Income to qualify	
	Amount	P & I		Monthly	Annual
$1,388	$108,800	$1,161	$136,000	$4,164	$49,963
$1,408	$110,400	$1,178	$138,000	$4,225	$50,698
$1,429	$112,000	$1,195	$140,000	$4,286	$51,432
$1,449	$113,600	$1,212	$142,000	$4,347	$52,167
$1,469	$115,200	$1,229	$144,000	$4,408	$52,902
$1,490	$116,800	$1,247	$146,000	$4,470	$53,637
$1,510	$118,400	$1,264	$148,000	$4,531	$54,371
$1,531	$120,000	$1,281	$150,000	$4,592	$55,106
$1,551	$121,600	$1,298	$152,000	$4,653	$55,841
$1,572	$123,200	$1,315	$154,000	$4,715	$56,576
$1,592	$124,800	$1,332	$156,000	$4,776	$57,310
$1,612	$126,400	$1,349	$158,000	$4,837	$58,045
$1,633	$128,000	$1,366	$160,000	$4,898	$58,780
$1,653	$129,600	$1,383	$162,000	$4,960	$59,515
$1,674	$131,200	$1,400	$164,000	$5,021	$60,249
$1,694	$132,800	$1,417	$166,000	$5,082	$60,984
$1,714	$134,400	$1,434	$168,000	$5,143	$61,719
$1,735	$136,000	$1,451	$170,000	$5,204	$62,454
$1,755	$137,600	$1,469	$172,000	$5,266	$63,188
$1,776	$139,200	$1,486	$174,000	$5,327	$63,923
$1,796	$140,800	$1,503	$176,000	$5,388	$64,658
$1,816	$142,400	$1,520	$178,000	$5,449	$65,393
$1,837	$144,000	$1,537	$180,000	$5,511	$66,127
$1,857	$145,600	$1,554	$182,000	$5,572	$66,862
$1,878	$147,200	$1,571	$184,000	$5,633	$67,597
$1,898	$148,800	$1,588	$186,000	$5,694	$68,332
$1,919	$150,400	$1,605	$188,000	$5,756	$69,066
$1,939	$152,000	$1,622	$190,000	$5,817	$69,801
$1,959	$153,600	$1,639	$192,000	$5,878	$70,536
$1,980	$155,200	$1,656	$194,000	$5,939	$71,271
$2,000	$156,800	$1,673	$196,000	$6,000	$72,005
$2,021	$158,400	$1,691	$198,000	$6,062	$72,740
$2,041	$160,000	$1,708	$200,000	$6,123	$73,475

13% Interest, 30-Year Term, 20% Down

(2% of purchase price assumed for taxes and insurance; 33% of gross monthly income allowed for mortgage payment)

Monthly payment	Maximum mortgage		Maximum price	Income to qualify	
	Amount	P & I		Monthly	Annual
$526	$40,000	$442	$50,000	$1,577	$18,929
$547	$41,600	$460	$52,000	$1,641	$19,687
$568	$43,200	$478	$54,000	$1,704	$20,444
$589	$44,800	$496	$56,000	$1,767	$21,201
$610	$46,400	$513	$58,000	$1,830	$21,958
$631	$48,000	$531	$60,000	$1,893	$22,715
$652	$49,600	$549	$62,000	$1,956	$23,472
$673	$51,200	$566	$64,000	$2,019	$24,230
$694	$52,800	$584	$66,000	$2,082	$24,987
$715	$54,400	$602	$68,000	$2,145	$25,744
$736	$56,000	$619	$70,000	$2,208	$26,501
$757	$57,600	$637	$72,000	$2,272	$27,258
$778	$59,200	$655	$74,000	$2,335	$28,016
$799	$60,800	$673	$76,000	$2,398	$28,773
$820	$62,400	$690	$78,000	$2,461	$29,530
$841	$64,000	$708	$80,000	$2,524	$30,287
$862	$65,600	$726	$82,000	$2,587	$31,044
$883	$67,200	$743	$84,000	$2,650	$31,801
$904	$68,800	$761	$86,000	$2,713	$32,559
$925	$70,400	$779	$88,000	$2,776	$33,316
$946	$72,000	$796	$90,000	$2,839	$34,073
$968	$73,600	$814	$92,000	$2,903	$34,830
$989	$75,200	$832	$94,000	$2,966	$35,587
$1,010	$76,800	$850	$96,000	$3,029	$36,344
$1,031	$78,400	$867	$98,000	$3,092	$37,102
$1,052	$80,000	$885	$100,000	$3,155	$37,859
$1,073	$81,600	$903	$102,000	$3,218	$38,616
$1,094	$83,200	$920	$104,000	$3,281	$39,373
$1,115	$84,800	$938	$106,000	$3,344	$40,130
$1,136	$86,400	$956	$108,000	$3,407	$40,888
$1,157	$88,000	$973	$110,000	$3,470	$41,645
$1,178	$89,600	$991	$112,000	$3,533	$42,402
$1,199	$91,200	$1,009	$114,000	$3,597	$43,159
$1,220	$92,800	$1,027	$116,000	$3,660	$43,916
$1,241	$94,400	$1,044	$118,000	$3,723	$44,673
$1,262	$96,000	$1,062	$120,000	$3,786	$45,431
$1,283	$97,600	$1,080	$122,000	$3,849	$46,188
$1,304	$99,200	$1,097	$124,000	$3,912	$46,945
$1,325	$100,800	$1,115	$126,000	$3,975	$47,702
$1,346	$102,400	$1,133	$128,000	$4,038	$48,459
$1,367	$104,000	$1,150	$130,000	$4,101	$49,217
$1,388	$105,600	$1,168	$132,000	$4,164	$49,974
$1,409	$107,200	$1,186	$134,000	$4,228	$50,731

Monthly payment	Maximum mortgage		Maximum price	Income to qualify	
	Amount	P & I		Monthly	Annual
$1,430	$108,800	$1,204	$136,000	$4,291	$51,488
$1,451	$110,400	$1,221	$138,000	$4,354	$52,245
$1,472	$112,000	$1,239	$140,000	$4,417	$53,002
$1,493	$113,600	$1,257	$142,000	$4,480	$53,760
$1,514	$115,200	$1,274	$144,000	$4,543	$54,517
$1,535	$116,800	$1,292	$146,000	$4,606	$55,274
$1,556	$118,400	$1,310	$148,000	$4,669	$56,031
$1,577	$120,000	$1,327	$150,000	$4,732	$56,788
$1,598	$121,600	$1,345	$152,000	$4,795	$57,545
$1,620	$123,200	$1,363	$154,000	$4,859	$58,303
$1,641	$124,800	$1,381	$156,000	$4,922	$59,060
$1,662	$126,400	$1,398	$158,000	$4,985	$59,817
$1,683	$128,000	$1,416	$160,000	$5,048	$60,574
$1,704	$129,600	$1,434	$162,000	$5,111	$61,331
$1,725	$131,200	$1,451	$164,000	$5,174	$62,089
$1,746	$132,800	$1,469	$166,000	$5,237	$62,846
$1,767	$134,400	$1,487	$168,000	$5,300	$63,603
$1,788	$136,000	$1,504	$170,000	$5,363	$64,360
$1,809	$137,600	$1,522	$172,000	$5,426	$65,117
$1,830	$139,200	$1,540	$174,000	$5,490	$65,874
$1,851	$140,800	$1,558	$176,000	$5,553	$66,632
$1,872	$142,400	$1,575	$178,000	$5,616	$67,389
$1,893	$144,000	$1,593	$180,000	$5,679	$68,146
$1,914	$145,600	$1,611	$182,000	$5,742	$68,903
$1,935	$147,200	$1,628	$184,000	$5,805	$69,660
$1,956	$148,800	$1,646	$186,000	$5,868	$70,417
$1,977	$150,400	$1,664	$188,000	$5,931	$71,175
$1,998	$152,000	$1,681	$190,000	$5,994	$71,932
$2,019	$153,600	$1,699	$192,000	$6,057	$72,689
$2,040	$155,200	$1,717	$194,000	$6,121	$73,446
$2,061	$156,800	$1,735	$196,000	$6,184	$74,203
$2,082	$158,400	$1,752	$198,000	$6,247	$74,961
$2,103	$160,000	$1,770	$200,000	$6,310	$75,718

13½% Interest, 30-Year Term, 20% Down

(2% of purchase price assumed for taxes and insurance; 33% of gross monthly income allowed for mortgage payment)

Monthly payment	Maximum mortgage		Maximum price	Income to qualify	
	Amount	P & I		Monthly	Annual
$542	$40,000	$458	$50,000	$1,625	$19,494
$563	$41,600	$476	$52,000	$1,689	$20,274
$585	$43,200	$495	$54,000	$1,754	$21,054
$606	$44,800	$513	$56,000	$1,819	$21,833
$628	$46,400	$531	$58,000	$1,884	$22,613
$650	$48,000	$550	$60,000	$1,949	$23,393
$671	$49,600	$568	$62,000	$2,014	$24,173
$693	$51,200	$586	$64,000	$2,079	$24,952
$715	$52,800	$605	$66,000	$2,144	$25,732
$736	$54,400	$623	$68,000	$2,209	$26,512
$758	$56,000	$641	$70,000	$2,274	$27,292
$780	$57,600	$660	$72,000	$2,339	$28,071
$801	$59,200	$678	$74,000	$2,404	$28,851
$823	$60,800	$696	$76,000	$2,469	$29,631
$845	$62,400	$715	$78,000	$2,534	$30,411
$866	$64,000	$733	$80,000	$2,599	$31,190
$888	$65,600	$751	$82,000	$2,664	$31,970
$910	$67,200	$770	$84,000	$2,729	$32,750
$931	$68,800	$788	$86,000	$2,794	$33,530
$953	$70,400	$806	$88,000	$2,859	$34,310
$975	$72,000	$825	$90,000	$2,924	$35,089
$996	$73,600	$843	$92,000	$2,989	$35,869
$1,018	$75,200	$861	$94,000	$3,054	$36,649
$1,040	$76,800	$880	$96,000	$3,119	$37,429
$1,061	$78,400	$898	$98,000	$3,184	$38,208
$1,083	$80,000	$916	$100,000	$3,249	$38,988
$1,105	$81,600	$935	$102,000	$3,314	$39,768
$1,126	$83,200	$953	$104,000	$3,379	$40,548
$1,148	$84,800	$971	$106,000	$3,444	$41,327
$1,170	$86,400	$990	$108,000	$3,509	$42,107
$1,191	$88,000	$1,008	$110,000	$3,574	$42,887
$1,213	$89,600	$1,026	$112,000	$3,639	$43,667
$1,235	$91,200	$1,045	$114,000	$3,704	$44,446
$1,256	$92,800	$1,063	$116,000	$3,769	$45,226
$1,278	$94,400	$1,081	$118,000	$3,834	$46,006
$1,300	$96,000	$1,100	$120,000	$3,899	$46,786
$1,321	$97,600	$1,118	$122,000	$3,964	$47,565
$1,343	$99,200	$1,136	$124,000	$4,029	$48,345
$1,365	$100,800	$1,155	$126,000	$4,094	$49,125
$1,386	$102,400	$1,173	$128,000	$4,159	$49,905
$1,408	$104,000	$1,191	$130,000	$4,224	$50,685
$1,430	$105,600	$1,210	$132,000	$4,289	$51,464
$1,451	$107,200	$1,228	$134,000	$4,354	$52,244

Monthly payment	Maximum mortgage		Maximum price	Income to qualify	
	Amount	P & I		Monthly	Annual
$1,473	$108,800	$1,246	$136,000	$4,419	$53,024
$1,495	$110,400	$1,265	$138,000	$4,484	$53,804
$1,516	$112,000	$1,283	$140,000	$4,549	$54,583
$1,538	$113,600	$1,301	$142,000	$4,614	$55,363
$1,560	$115,200	$1,320	$144,000	$4,679	$56,143
$1,581	$116,800	$1,338	$146,000	$4,744	$56,923
$1,603	$118,400	$1,356	$148,000	$4,809	$57,702
$1,625	$120,000	$1,375	$150,000	$4,874	$58,482
$1,646	$121,600	$1,393	$152,000	$4,938	$59,262
$1,668	$123,200	$1,411	$154,000	$5,003	$60,042
$1,689	$124,800	$1,429	$156,000	$5,068	$60,821
$1,711	$126,400	$1,448	$158,000	$5,133	$61,601
$1,733	$128,000	$1,466	$160,000	$5,198	$62,381
$1,754	$129,600	$1,484	$162,000	$5,263	$63,161
$1,776	$131,200	$1,503	$164,000	$5,328	$63,940
$1,798	$132,800	$1,521	$166,000	$5,393	$64,720
$1,819	$134,400	$1,539	$168,000	$5,458	$65,500
$1,841	$136,000	$1,558	$170,000	$5,523	$66,280
$1,863	$137,600	$1,576	$172,000	$5,588	$67,060
$1,884	$139,200	$1,594	$174,000	$5,653	$67,839
$1,906	$140,800	$1,613	$176,000	$5,718	$68,619
$1,928	$142,400	$1,631	$178,000	$5,783	$69,399
$1,949	$144,000	$1,649	$180,000	$5,848	$70,179
$1,971	$145,600	$1,668	$182,000	$5,913	$70,958
$1,993	$147,200	$1,686	$184,000	$5,978	$71,738
$2,014	$148,800	$1,704	$186,000	$6,043	$72,518
$2,036	$150,400	$1,723	$188,000	$6,108	$73,298
$2,058	$152,000	$1,741	$190,000	$6,173	$74,077
$2,079	$153,600	$1,759	$192,000	$6,238	$74,857
$2,101	$155,200	$1,778	$194,000	$6,303	$75,637
$2,123	$156,800	$1,796	$196,000	$6,368	$76,417
$2,144	$158,400	$1,814	$198,000	$6,433	$77,196
$2,166	$160,000	$1,833	$200,000	$6,498	$77,976

14% Interest, 30-Year Term, 20% Down

(2% of purchase price assumed for taxes and insurance; 33% of gross monthly income allowed for mortgage payment)

Monthly payment	Maximum mortgage		Maximum price	Income to qualify	
	Amount	P & I		Monthly	Annual
$557	$40,000	$474	$50,000	$1,672	$20,062
$580	$41,600	$493	$52,000	$1,739	$20,865
$602	$43,200	$512	$54,000	$1,806	$21,667
$624	$44,800	$531	$56,000	$1,872	$22,470
$646	$46,400	$550	$58,000	$1,939	$23,272
$669	$48,000	$569	$60,000	$2,006	$24,075
$691	$49,600	$588	$62,000	$2,073	$24,877
$713	$51,200	$607	$64,000	$2,140	$25,680
$736	$52,800	$626	$66,000	$2,207	$26,482
$758	$54,400	$645	$68,000	$2,274	$27,285
$780	$56,000	$664	$70,000	$2,341	$28,087
$802	$57,600	$682	$72,000	$2,407	$28,890
$825	$59,200	$701	$74,000	$2,474	$29,692
$847	$60,800	$720	$76,000	$2,541	$30,495
$869	$62,400	$739	$78,000	$2,608	$31,297
$892	$64,000	$758	$80,000	$2,675	$32,100
$914	$65,600	$777	$82,000	$2,742	$32,902
$936	$67,200	$796	$84,000	$2,809	$33,705
$959	$68,800	$815	$86,000	$2,876	$34,507
$981	$70,400	$834	$88,000	$2,942	$35,310
$1,003	$72,000	$853	$90,000	$3,009	$36,112
$1,025	$73,600	$872	$92,000	$3,076	$36,915
$1,048	$75,200	$891	$94,000	$3,143	$37,717
$1,070	$76,800	$910	$96,000	$3,210	$38,520
$1,092	$78,400	$929	$98,000	$3,277	$39,322
$1,115	$80,000	$948	$100,000	$3,344	$40,125
$1,137	$81,600	$967	$102,000	$3,411	$40,927
$1,159	$83,200	$986	$104,000	$3,477	$41,730
$1,181	$84,800	$1,005	$106,000	$3,544	$42,532
$1,204	$86,400	$1,024	$108,000	$3,611	$43,335
$1,226	$88,000	$1,043	$110,000	$3,678	$44,137
$1,248	$89,600	$1,062	$112,000	$3,745	$44,939
$1,271	$91,200	$1,081	$114,000	$3,812	$45,742
$1,293	$92,800	$1,100	$116,000	$3,879	$46,544
$1,315	$94,400	$1,119	$118,000	$3,946	$47,347
$1,337	$96,000	$1,137	$120,000	$4,012	$48,149
$1,360	$97,600	$1,156	$122,000	$4,079	$48,952
$1,382	$99,200	$1,175	$124,000	$4,146	$49,754
$1,404	$100,800	$1,194	$126,000	$4,213	$50,557
$1,427	$102,400	$1,213	$128,000	$4,280	$51,359
$1,449	$104,000	$1,232	$130,000	$4,347	$52,162
$1,471	$105,600	$1,251	$132,000	$4,414	$52,964
$1,494	$107,200	$1,270	$134,000	$4,481	$53,767

Monthly payment	Maximum mortgage		Maximum price	Income to qualify	
	Amount	P & I		Monthly	Annual
$1,516	$108,800	$1,289	$136,000	$4,547	$54,569
$1,538	$110,400	$1,308	$138,000	$4,614	$55,372
$1,560	$112,000	$1,327	$140,000	$4,681	$56,174
$1,583	$113,600	$1,346	$142,000	$4,748	$56,977
$1,605	$115,200	$1,365	$144,000	$4,815	$57,779
$1,627	$116,800	$1,384	$146,000	$4,882	$58,582
$1,650	$118,400	$1,403	$148,000	$4,949	$59,384
$1,672	$120,000	$1,422	$150,000	$5,016	$60,187
$1,694	$121,600	$1,441	$152,000	$5,082	$60,989
$1,716	$123,200	$1,460	$154,000	$5,149	$61,792
$1,739	$124,800	$1,479	$156,000	$5,216	$62,594
$1,761	$126,400	$1,498	$158,000	$5,283	$63,397
$1,783	$128,000	$1,517	$160,000	$5,350	$64,199
$1,806	$129,600	$1,536	$162,000	$5,417	$65,002
$1,828	$131,200	$1,555	$164,000	$5,484	$65,804
$1,850	$132,800	$1,574	$166,000	$5,551	$66,607
$1,872	$134,400	$1,592	$168,000	$5,617	$67,409
$1,895	$136,000	$1,611	$170,000	$5,684	$68,212
$1,917	$137,600	$1,630	$172,000	$5,751	$69,014
$1,939	$139,200	$1,649	$174,000	$5,818	$69,817
$1,962	$140,800	$1,668	$176,000	$5,885	$70,619
$1,984	$142,400	$1,687	$178,000	$5,952	$71,422
$2,006	$144,000	$1,706	$180,000	$6,019	$72,224
$2,029	$145,600	$1,725	$182,000	$6,086	$73,027
$2,051	$147,200	$1,744	$184,000	$6,152	$73,829
$2,073	$148,800	$1,763	$186,000	$6,219	$74,632
$2,095	$150,400	$1,782	$188,000	$6,286	$75,434
$2,118	$152,000	$1,801	$190,000	$6,353	$76,237
$2,140	$153,600	$1,820	$192,000	$6,420	$77,039
$2,162	$155,200	$1,839	$194,000	$6,487	$77,842
$2,185	$156,800	$1,858	$196,000	$6,554	$78,644
$2,207	$158,400	$1,877	$198,000	$6,621	$79,447
$2,229	$160,000	$1,896	$200,000	$6,687	$80,249

14½% Interest, 30-Year Term, 20% Down

(2% of purchase price assumed for taxes and insurance; 33% of gross monthly income allowed for mortgage payment)

Monthly payment	Maximum mortgage		Maximum price	Income to qualify	
	Amount	P & I		Monthly	Annual
$573	$40,000	$490	$50,000	$1,719	$20,634
$596	$41,600	$509	$52,000	$1,788	$21,459
$619	$43,200	$529	$54,000	$1,857	$22,284
$642	$44,800	$549	$56,000	$1,926	$23,110
$665	$46,400	$568	$58,000	$1,995	$23,935
$688	$48,000	$588	$60,000	$2,063	$24,760
$711	$49,600	$607	$62,000	$2,132	$25,586
$734	$51,200	$627	$64,000	$2,201	$26,411
$757	$52,800	$647	$66,000	$2,270	$27,236
$779	$54,400	$666	$68,000	$2,338	$28,062
$802	$56,000	$686	$70,000	$2,407	$28,887
$825	$57,600	$705	$72,000	$2,476	$29,712
$848	$59,200	$725	$74,000	$2,545	$30,538
$871	$60,800	$745	$76,000	$2,614	$31,363
$894	$62,400	$764	$78,000	$2,682	$32,189
$917	$64,000	$784	$80,000	$2,751	$33,014
$940	$65,600	$803	$82,000	$2,820	$33,839
$963	$67,200	$823	$84,000	$2,889	$34,665
$986	$68,800	$842	$86,000	$2,957	$35,490
$1,009	$70,400	$862	$88,000	$3,026	$36,315
$1,032	$72,000	$882	$90,000	$3,095	$37,141
$1,055	$73,600	$901	$92,000	$3,164	$37,966
$1,078	$75,200	$921	$94,000	$3,233	$38,791
$1,100	$76,800	$940	$96,000	$3,301	$39,617
$1,123	$78,400	$960	$98,000	$3,370	$40,442
$1,146	$80,000	$980	$100,000	$3,439	$41,267
$1,169	$81,600	$999	$102,000	$3,508	$42,093
$1,192	$83,200	$1,019	$104,000	$3,577	$42,918
$1,215	$84,800	$1,038	$106,000	$3,645	$43,743
$1,238	$86,400	$1,058	$108,000	$3,714	$44,569
$1,261	$88,000	$1,078	$110,000	$3,783	$45,394
$1,284	$89,600	$1,097	$112,000	$3,852	$46,219
$1,307	$91,200	$1,117	$114,000	$3,920	$47,045
$1,330	$92,800	$1,136	$116,000	$3,989	$47,870
$1,353	$94,400	$1,156	$118,000	$4,058	$48,695
$1,376	$96,000	$1,176	$120,000	$4,127	$49,521
$1,399	$97,600	$1,195	$122,000	$4,196	$50,346
$1,421	$99,200	$1,215	$124,000	$4,264	$51,171
$1,444	$100,800	$1,234	$126,000	$4,333	$51,997
$1,467	$102,400	$1,254	$128,000	$4,402	$52,822
$1,490	$104,000	$1,274	$130,000	$4,471	$53,648
$1,513	$105,600	$1,293	$132,000	$4,539	$54,473
$1,536	$107,200	$1,313	$134,000	$4,608	$55,298

Monthly payment	Maximum mortgage		Maximum price	Income to qualify	
	Amount	P & I		Monthly	Annual
$1,559	$108,800	$1,332	$136,000	$4,677	$56,124
$1,582	$110,400	$1,352	$138,000	$4,746	$56,949
$1,605	$112,000	$1,372	$140,000	$4,815	$57,774
$1,628	$113,600	$1,391	$142,000	$4,883	$58,600
$1,651	$115,200	$1,411	$144,000	$4,952	$59,425
$1,674	$116,800	$1,430	$146,000	$5,021	$60,250
$1,697	$118,400	$1,450	$148,000	$5,090	$61,076
$1,719	$120,000	$1,469	$150,000	$5,158	$61,901
$1,742	$121,600	$1,489	$152,000	$5,227	$62,726
$1,765	$123,200	$1,509	$154,000	$5,296	$63,552
$1,788	$124,800	$1,528	$156,000	$5,365	$64,377
$1,811	$126,400	$1,548	$158,000	$5,434	$65,202
$1,834	$128,000	$1,567	$160,000	$5,502	$66,028
$1,857	$129,600	$1,587	$162,000	$5,571	$66,853
$1,880	$131,200	$1,607	$164,000	$5,640	$67,678
$1,903	$132,800	$1,626	$166,000	$5,709	$68,504
$1,926	$134,400	$1,646	$168,000	$5,777	$69,329
$1,949	$136,000	$1,665	$170,000	$5,846	$70,154
$1,972	$137,600	$1,685	$172,000	$5,915	$70,980
$1,995	$139,200	$1,705	$174,000	$5,984	$71,805
$2,018	$140,800	$1,724	$176,000	$6,053	$72,630
$2,040	$142,400	$1,744	$178,000	$6,121	$73,456
$2,063	$144,000	$1,763	$180,000	$6,190	$74,281
$2,086	$145,600	$1,783	$182,000	$6,259	$75,107
$2,109	$147,200	$1,803	$184,000	$6,328	$75,932
$2,132	$148,800	$1,822	$186,000	$6,396	$76,757
$2,155	$150,400	$1,842	$188,000	$6,465	$77,583
$2,178	$152,000	$1,861	$190,000	$6,534	$78,408
$2,201	$153,600	$1,881	$192,000	$6,603	$79,233
$2,224	$155,200	$1,901	$194,000	$6,672	$80,059
$2,247	$156,800	$1,920	$196,000	$6,740	$80,884
$2,270	$158,400	$1,940	$198,000	$6,809	$81,709
$2,293	$160,000	$1,959	$200,000	$6,878	$82,535

15% Interest, 30-Year Term, 20% Down

(2% of purchase price assumed for taxes and insurance; 33% of gross monthly income allowed for mortgage payment)

Monthly payment	Maximum mortgage		Maximum price	Income to qualify	
	Amount	P & I		Monthly	Annual
$589	$40,000	$506	$50,000	$1,767	$21,208
$613	$41,600	$526	$52,000	$1,838	$22,056
$636	$43,200	$546	$54,000	$1,909	$22,905
$660	$44,800	$566	$56,000	$1,979	$23,753
$683	$46,400	$587	$58,000	$2,050	$24,601
$707	$48,000	$607	$60,000	$2,121	$25,450
$731	$49,600	$627	$62,000	$2,192	$26,298
$754	$51,200	$647	$64,000	$2,262	$27,146
$778	$52,800	$668	$66,000	$2,333	$27,995
$801	$54,400	$688	$68,000	$2,404	$28,843
$825	$56,000	$708	$70,000	$2,474	$29,691
$848	$57,600	$728	$72,000	$2,545	$30,540
$872	$59,200	$749	$74,000	$2,616	$31,388
$895	$60,800	$769	$76,000	$2,686	$32,236
$919	$62,400	$789	$78,000	$2,757	$33,085
$943	$64,000	$809	$80,000	$2,828	$33,933
$966	$65,600	$829	$82,000	$2,898	$34,781
$990	$67,200	$850	$84,000	$2,969	$35,630
$1,013	$68,800	$870	$86,000	$3,040	$36,478
$1,037	$70,400	$890	$88,000	$3,111	$37,326
$1,060	$72,000	$910	$90,000	$3,181	$38,175
$1,084	$73,600	$931	$92,000	$3,252	$39,023
$1,108	$75,200	$951	$94,000	$3,323	$39,871
$1,131	$76,800	$971	$96,000	$3,393	$40,720
$1,155	$78,400	$991	$98,000	$3,464	$41,568
$1,178	$80,000	$1,012	$100,000	$3,535	$42,416
$1,202	$81,600	$1,032	$102,000	$3,605	$43,264
$1,225	$83,200	$1,052	$104,000	$3,676	$44,113
$1,249	$84,800	$1,072	$106,000	$3,747	$44,961
$1,272	$86,400	$1,092	$108,000	$3,817	$45,809
$1,296	$88,000	$1,113	$110,000	$3,888	$46,658
$1,320	$89,600	$1,133	$112,000	$3,959	$47,506
$1,343	$91,200	$1,153	$114,000	$4,030	$48,354
$1,367	$92,800	$1,173	$116,000	$4,100	$49,203
$1,390	$94,400	$1,194	$118,000	$4,171	$50,051
$1,414	$96,000	$1,214	$120,000	$4,242	$50,899
$1,437	$97,600	$1,234	$122,000	$4,312	$51,748
$1,461	$99,200	$1,254	$124,000	$4,383	$52,596
$1,485	$100,800	$1,275	$126,000	$4,454	$53,444
$1,508	$102,400	$1,295	$128,000	$4,524	$54,293
$1,532	$104,000	$1,315	$130,000	$4,595	$55,141
$1,555	$105,600	$1,335	$132,000	$4,666	$55,989
$1,579	$107,200	$1,355	$134,000	$4,736	$56,838

Monthly payment	Maximum mortgage		Maximum price	Income to qualify	
	Amount	P & I		Monthly	Annual
$1,602	$108,800	$1,376	$136,000	$4,807	$57,686
$1,626	$110,400	$1,396	$138,000	$4,878	$58,534
$1,650	$112,000	$1,416	$140,000	$4,949	$59,383
$1,673	$113,600	$1,436	$142,000	$5,019	$60,231
$1,697	$115,200	$1,457	$144,000	$5,090	$61,079
$1,720	$116,800	$1,477	$146,000	$5,161	$61,928
$1,744	$118,400	$1,497	$148,000	$5,231	$62,776
$1,767	$120,000	$1,517	$150,000	$5,302	$63,624
$1,791	$121,600	$1,538	$152,000	$5,373	$64,473
$1,814	$123,200	$1,558	$154,000	$5,443	$65,321
$1,838	$124,800	$1,578	$156,000	$5,514	$66,169
$1,862	$126,400	$1,598	$158,000	$5,585	$67,018
$1,885	$128,000	$1,618	$160,000	$5,655	$67,866
$1,909	$129,600	$1,639	$162,000	$5,726	$68,714
$1,932	$131,200	$1,659	$164,000	$5,797	$69,563
$1,956	$132,800	$1,679	$166,000	$5,868	$70,411
$1,979	$134,400	$1,699	$168,000	$5,938	$71,259
$2,003	$136,000	$1,720	$170,000	$6,009	$72,107
$2,027	$137,600	$1,740	$172,000	$6,080	$72,956
$2,050	$139,200	$1,760	$174,000	$6,150	$73,804
$2,074	$140,800	$1,780	$176,000	$6,221	$74,652
$2,097	$142,400	$1,801	$178,000	$6,292	$75,501
$2,121	$144,000	$1,821	$180,000	$6,362	$76,349
$2,144	$145,600	$1,841	$182,000	$6,433	$77,197
$2,168	$147,200	$1,861	$184,000	$6,504	$78,046
$2,192	$148,800	$1,882	$186,000	$6,575	$78,894
$2,215	$150,400	$1,902	$188,000	$6,645	$79,742
$2,239	$152,000	$1,922	$190,000	$6,716	$80,591
$2,262	$153,600	$1,942	$192,000	$6,787	$81,439
$2,286	$155,200	$1,962	$194,000	$6,857	$82,287
$2,309	$156,800	$1,983	$196,000	$6,928	$83,136
$2,333	$158,400	$2,003	$198,000	$6,999	$83,984
$2,356	$160,000	$2,023	$200,000	$7,069	$84,832

Index

About the Author

Robert Irwin is one of the best-known authors in real estate. He has been a successful California real estate broker for over 25 years, guiding many buyers and sellers through a variety of profitable real estate transactions. He has served as a consultant to lenders, investors, and other brokers, helping to secure financing for transactions that might otherwise not have been made. Mr. Irwin is also a highly successful private real estate investor and has written and edited nearly a dozen important books on real estate for McGraw-Hill, including *How to Find Hidden Real Estate Bargains* (1986), the *Handbook of Property Management* (1986), *Computerizing Your Real Estate Office* (1985), *The McGraw-Hill Real Estate Handbook* (1984), and *The New Mortgage Game* (1982), as this book was formerly titled.